PRAISE for *REMOTE LEADERSHIP*

This book will help managers to become better and more effective remote managers, because of the many tips and useful checklists it contains.

Philip Todd
Past Director of the Netherlands Telework Forum

Research by the authors of *Remote Leadership* validates that employees will continue to prefer some degree of flexibility to work remotely beyond the pandemic. The authors help you prepare for the ongoing issues remote teams present for leaders and their organizations. You have likely encountered the difficulty of clear, correct communication in a remote environment, and the authors provide practical recommendations you can implement. In addition, they address more challenging issues you face, such as hiring virtually, maintaining your organization's culture, and the best way to build trust remotely. *Remote Leadership* is so packed with tools and solutions that you'll want to start another remote team just to try them out.

Elaine Biech
President, ebb associates inc

The content was well organized and relevant. Every time I said to myself "this point is good but what about culture, or people or onboarding?" sure enough the topic would show up in a subsequent chapter. This book covered the employee life cycle as it relates to remote leadership. This is full of helpful hints and tools. I would recommend this to anyone.

Joe Ann Smith
Head of Human Resources and
Organizational Development (acting)
Eppendorf Group

Dinnocenzo and Morwick have pulled together a terrific resource with this book. I've been helping organizations adopt and optimize remote and flexible work strategies for over fifteen years and I still learned a lot from *Remote Leadership*. The genie is out of the bottle on remote work, and it's not going back in. Those that were new to it at the start of the pandemic have learned a lot in a very short period of time, but if they want to optimize the potential of a flexible strategy, they will be wise to read this book.

Kate Lister
President of Global Workplace Analytics
—one of the most respected names in the future of work

Both engaging and practical, Dinnocenzo & Morwick provide best practices, relatable examples, and useful tips and techniques. Both experienced leaders and those new to remote leadership will find value here in meeting the challenges of leading from a distance.

David K. Milliken
Managing Partner, Blueline Simulations, LLC

This is a thorough and comprehensive review of the opportunities, issues, and challenges surrounding remote work and the strategies required for effective, high-impact leadership in the "new normal" of leading from a distance. It serves as a checklist of strategies and tactics for leaders to not just maintain, but even increase, their impact and effectiveness.

David Binder
Talent Management Consultant

Remote Leadership is an excellent book to read for the effective management of distributed workplace. Dinnocenzo & Morwick share their deep expertise in workplace strategy and remote work while leveraging insightful data that equips leaders with the skills to manage an evolving and exciting workplace of the future, one that is dynamic, fluid and hybrid.

Emily Klein
Director of Workplace, Perkins&Will and co-author of Workshift:
Future-Proof Your Organization for the 21st Century

While I no longer contribute to the economy, I can easily see where a manger might find these tips and techniques quite valuable. Obviously the creative/destructive force released into our world in 2020 provides an enormous opportunity for those able to harness its energy. Sadly, most leaders will miss this moment of extreme opportunity. Remote Leadership will serve as a wake-up call for those with nostalgia for 2019.

William A. Branch
Serial Entrepreneur

Remote Leadership takes life and work online to a new level. It is filled with suggestions, techniques, principles, personal anecdotes, and, most importantly, a common-sense approach to virtual minefields. A roadmap for not only online workers, but also everyone involved in virtual groups, it is a handbook you'll want to keep close as you navigate the new normal.

Prudence Spink
Attorney

Dinnocenzo and Morwick bring clarity to the opportunities and challenges associated with remote work. From defining hybrid teams to building a 'remote-first culture,' and presenting the case for 'remote work as a catalyst for innovating,' they provide practical, easy-to-implement tips for improving performance as more and more teams work from a distance."

Laura A. Grover
F-500 Senior Director Digital Strategy

Remote Leadership is a must-read for leaders who manage remote workers. Comprehensive in its approach, the book is also a guide to the skills needed to be successful in working with employees who are located away from the leader. Remote workers will also benefit from reading this book so that they understand the challenges their leaders face and what to expect from an enlightened leader.

Joan Schwetz
Consultant, Sales Whizdom

This is a quick and easy read for us "timed strapped" folks. The tables and charts at the end enable one to put the excellent material contained in the book quickly into action. As someone who has served on a variety of boards for decades and currently is chairman of several, the era of virtual meetings is upon us and is here to stay. *Remote Leadership* is the best I have read on how to organize and conduct those meetings to achieve the greatest success.

Richard S. Hamilton
Chairman AAA East Central; Vice Chairman, Automobile
Club of Southern California; Chairman, UPMC Passavant and
UPMC St. Margaret Hospitals

The COVID-19 pandemic has accelerated a dramatic change in the deployment of business workers that had already begun. Remote work is a fact of life. Any business leaders who want to understand and successfully adopt remote work to support strategic goals of their business must read *Remote Leadership* and keep it close at hand. It is a thoughtful, comprehensive, and very practical management tool that will show any business with remote workers how to 'stay ahead of the curve' and maximize the benefits of this non-traditional but increasingly utilized business model.

Jay A. Summerville
Ordained Pastor, Presbyterian Church (USA)

As a novice in remote management, I found this book to be both instructional and insightful. I think the content could be very useful to teachers who are likely to increasingly teach remotely. Granted, students are not employees, but many of the ideas presented here on remote management could support better student engagement. The section on inquiring about the student's (employee's) family or a non-work topic is an especially important way for a teacher to connect. Taking time to send a quick email or text to check in can make a difference in a student's motivation. Granted, the number of students a teacher has might limit frequent contacts, but often the smallest recognition can make a big difference.

Melissa Carl
Retired Educator

REMOTE LEADERSHIP

SUCCESSFULLY LEADING
WORK-FROM-ANYWHERE AND HYBRID TEAMS

REMOTE LEADERSHIP

SUCCESSFULLY LEADING
WORK-FROM-ANYWHERE AND HYBRID TEAMS

DEBRA A. DINNOCENZO & JASON MORWICK

Published by:

The WALK THE TALK® Company
P.O. Box 210996
Bedford, Texas 76095

Library of Congress Cataloging-in-Publication Data:
ISBN: 978-1-885228-15-4   Perfect Bound

To order additional copies or inquiries regarding permission the material contained in *Remote Leadership*, please visit:
www.remoteleadershipbook.com

Also available on Amazon

Printed and bound in the United States of America

26   25   24   23   22   21   1   2   3   4   5   6   7 8

DEDICATION

For Rick Swegan,
my life and work partner
always there for me,
and my most enduring supporter.
D.D.

For Genie,
my partner and best friend,
for your endless support and encouragement.
J.M.

CONTENTS

ACKNOWLEDGMENTS

Even though you're reading this near the beginning, it was the last section we wrote—following the long march from "Hey, why don't we write a book?" to the end result. It's been an exciting, (mostly) fun, and challenging journey, made possible by many people who have supported the effort through a variety of contributions.

While you see the names of only two authors, we've had partners who have been vital to this book becoming a reality. So, first and foremost, we want to thank our spouses and life partners, Rick Swegan and Genie Morwick, for their willingness to handle all the other stuff of life and to be cheerleaders, readers, and good sports about it all.

We are thrilled to have the wisdom and experience of two industry giants included in our book. Jack Nilles, without whom the term "telecommuting" may have never been coined, has written the Retrospective, an important look at how remote work has evolved. And Jack Zenger, a renowned leadership and training expert, provides an important perspective in the Foreword. We offer our thanks to both for their invaluable contributions.

Many other people have shared their experience and feedback as we moved through research, writing, editing, and publishing. We thank them all for their time, insights, and comments that have made this a better book.

❖ While we can't name them all, we're very appreciative of the hundreds of people who responded to our surveys. Their voices are heard throughout the book, and their experiences enrich the content.

❖ A small army of supporters took even more time to participate in interviews or to review the manuscript. We received from each of them much value in developing content that is relevant to the challenges leaders face in the expanding remote workplace. We offer our sincere thanks to Thomas Ashley, Dennis Barger, Robert Barnes, Elaine Biech, Evan Carl, Melissa Carl, David Binder, William Branch, Mark Elliott, Jim Ford, Michael Forst, Laura Grover, Richard Hamilton, Josh Kennedy, Emily Klein, David Milliken, Milo Paich, Richard Parlato, Alice Pescuric, Tim Renjilian, Joan Schwetz, Joe Ann Smith, Prudence Spink, Jay Summerville, and Philip Todd.

❖ Moving the book from a bunch of words to an error-free printed volume is a result of the great support from amazing partners. We offer our deep gratitude to Erika Westmoreland (Walk The Talk) and Melissa Farr (Back Porch Creative) – two of the most incredible MAKE IT HAPPEN people on the planet!

❖ And thanks to you for reading our book and for your commitment to the value of learning. We hope our book makes a difference in your success as a remote leader.

OTHER BOOKS BY THE AUTHORS

Debra A. Dinnocenzo

How to Lead from a Distance

Working from a Distance

101 Tips for Telecommuters

Managing Telecommuters

Emergency Telecommuting

Dot Calm: The Search for Sanity in a Wired World
  (with Richard B. Swegan)

Working Too Much Can Make You Grumpy

Jason Morwick

Making Telework Work
  (with Evan H. Offstein)

Workshift: Future-Proof Your Organization for the 21st Century
  (with Robyn Bews, Emily Klein & Tim Lorman)

Gridiron Leadership: Winning Strategies and Breakthrough Tactics
  (with Evan H. Offstein & Scott Griffith)

.

RETROSPECTIVE

From the Father of Telecommuting

THE BEGINNING

In the 1960s and early 1970s - those were my rocket scientist days - I often wondered how the technology we used for space could be applied to real world situations. As part of my search in 1971, I came across a regional planner who said to me, "If you people can put a man on the moon, then why can't you do something about traffic? Why can't you just keep people off the freeways?" It was a revelation to me. Why not indeed?

I started to examine the problem from first principles. Why do we have traffic, particularly rush-hour traffic? It turned out that a large proportion of rush-hour traffic comprises people driving to or from their homes and their workplaces. What do they do when they get to their workplaces? A little research showed that almost half of them were working in offices. What do they do when they get to their offices? A substantial amount of their time, at least in 1971, was spent on the phone talking to someone somewhere else.

If that's the case, I thought, then why can't they just phone from home and save the trips, not to mention gas costs, air pollution and depreciation to their cars?

At this same time I also happened to be the Secretary of my engineering company's research committee. I asked the committee members to spend some effort and funds on the idea of substituting telecommunications (the telephone) for transportation. They asked me what I would need to do the research. I said we would probably need to hire a psychologist or two and maybe an economist - we already had many engineers - to examine the implications of this rearrangement of work. Their response was disappointing. "We are an engineering company. We don't want to deal with this touchy-feely stuff." I could not convince them otherwise.

I was complaining about this reaction to a friend of mine who taught in the School of Engineering at the University of Southern California. I told him that USC had the right kind of people to do this research whereas my engineering company did not. Shortly thereafter, I repeated my assessment to the Executive Vice President of the university. He asked, "Why don't you do it here?" So I left the engineering company and went to USC to become its first director of Interdisciplinary Program Development.

As part of that job, I applied to the National Science Foundation for a grant entitled Development of Policy on the Telecommunications-Transportation Tradeoff. I got the grant and my chance to test my ideas in the real world. My team, comprising university faculty from the Schools of Engineering, Communication, and Business, enlisted the support of a major national insurance company to try distributing its workers into satellite offices near where they lived instead of having them come into the downtown offices every day. The project ran from 1973 to 1974 and was a resounding success. Worker productivity and job satisfaction increased, along with other positive indicators.

Early in the project I decided to call the process telecommuting or teleworking, depending on the audience, to make it more understandable to people than the telecommunications-transportation tradeoff. A book based on the project was published in 1976 in the US and 1977 in Japan.

To my dismay, the project did not continue. The company management was concerned that, with their workforce scattered around the region, it would be too easy for them to unionize. A few months later, I spoke with a planner for the AFL/CIO about our research. He too said that telecommuting was a terrible idea. Why? Because, if the workers were scattered all over the region, how could they be organized by the union? Both rejected telecommuting but for opposite reasons. I was getting the idea that telecommuting might be a bit too radical for both groups.

THE MIDDLE

Then began a series of requests for research funding, trials, and demonstrations of telecommuting in the real world. In the 1980s we enlisted the support of a number of Fortune 100 companies, many of which adopted telecommuting for their own employees. While giving us data on how well telecommuting was working in large US corporations, those projects produced another problem. Like the initial project with the insurance company, we were not allowed to divulge the names of our participants.

Meanwhile the technology of the telecommunications infrastructure was rapidly improving. In 1973 the option for telecommuting from home was out of the question since the telephone system could not handle the necessary bandwidths at a reasonable price. With the introduction of the IBM PC in 1981, the technology landscape suddenly grew brighter for home-based telecommuting. The PC provided the office at home while faster modems allowed ever easier communications to the traditional office.

Yet we still had the same fundamental problem in expanding the use of telecommuting. We quickly learned that enlisting potential telecommuters was no problem. However, attracting their management was another issue altogether since we couldn't point to specific companies to say, "The Xers have adopted telecommuting and are enthusiastic about it." We would point out telecommuting's improvements in productivity, reduced use of sick leave, and diminished facilities costs for very little in up-front investment. Often the response was, "It may work for X, but it won't work for us."

Frustrated by all this reluctance, we tried another tack by going to government agencies. With governments involved in telecommuting we could run the demonstration projects and release the data publicly! In the late 1980s and early 1990s we and others had successful projects with state and municipal governments. Even the federal government! After these projects, several people were ready to design and run successful telework projects in industry and government. We knew how to manage them successfully. I even wrote some books on the details; foremost among them is Managing Telework: Strategies for Managing the Virtual Workforce. I and my wife, Laila, spent considerable time in Europe and Asia in the 1990s giving presentations about telework.

Still the other shoe didn't drop, as the saying goes. Many managers were still reluctant to take a chance on telecommuting. After all, what you know now may be troublesome, but something new might be worse. Risk aversion was endemic except in many small- to medium-sized startups that got the message beginning in the 1980s. Even IBM and Yahoo gave up telework in the 21st century, largely because of management mistakes (in my opinion).

So, what could be the secret sauce that would grab the attention of CEOs everywhere?

THE DAWN, AMONG OTHER THINGS, BREAKS

The secret sauce turned out to be a microscopic virus called COVID-19. Essentially overnight the world has learned how important it is to keep people isolated from each other in order to avoid becoming infected with a severe, often fatal, disease. For roughly half the workforces in developed countries, telework, alias remote work, has become the key to survival.

Even so, my first thought in March 2020 focused on those millions of people, managers, and teleworkers alike, who have been thrust into teleworking without a clue as to how to do it. The vaccines are coming, this panic will abate, so do we wait until it's back to business as it was?

I think not. Serious evidence is growing that a substantial number of these newly bred teleworkers like it just fine and do not want to go back to that 20th century office environment – at least not full time. The workspace of the future is a different concept than yesterday's cacophonous rows of cubicles. The successful management of the future is not necessarily what you are used to. But you may enjoy it more.

Read on.

Jack M. Nilles
Los Angeles, California
December 2020

FOREWORD

Why Every Leader Should Read This Book

In my lifetime there have been some important shifts in people's beliefs and behavior. None comes even close to the dramatic shift that has occurred to one of the most fundamental elements of most people's life---the nature and location of their work.

Prior to 2020, roughly 16% of the US workforce worked from home. Beginning in the first quarter of 2020 that number swiftly jumped up. Some estimate that it is now 42%, while others have estimated that the number may be as high as 60%. Imagine that what had been 1 in 8 employees working remotely, now has become 4 to 6 out of 10. Employees who used to say in the morning, "I'm going to work" to describe the destination   to which they would commute, are now saying the same thing as they head toward the bedroom that has been converted into an office.

But this sudden and profound shift is not the only reason why every leader should read this book. There are few serious observers of this trend who believe this genie will ever be put back into its bottle. Surveys show that 80% of workers want to continue being able to work from home some of the time. Therefore, the challenges of managing a group of people who work remotely from you is the new reality for a huge part of what leaders will face in the future. And even more challenging than managing a group of people who are all physically remote, is the prospect of managing a group of subordinates comprised of some who are remote and some who are co-located with their leader.

What stands out about this book is its sheer practicality. The authors have conducted extensive research, building on their already extensive experience with this topic. The reader is given a complete immersion in the complex issues that this pattern of work creates. Better yet, this book provides practical solutions and recommendations for how to cope.

You will read useful solutions for coping with the broad underlying foundational issues of every organization—trust, communication and being present—but seen through the lens of this new pattern of work. Virtually every issue on the human side of remote leadership is addressed, along with practical solutions for it. The topics not covered here include the thornier and evolving issues for managers and organizations—such as tax, legal, and security matters that will impact remote work in the future. As these areas are addressed and resolved going forward, leaders will, in the meantime, find answers to nearly everything else from Dinnocenzo & Morwick.

Your time will be well spent in devouring this highly relevant book.

Jack Zenger
Co-founder & CEO, Zenger Folkman
Co-author of *The Extraordinary Leader: Turning Good Managers into Great Leaders*
Orem, Utah
December 2020

AUTHORS' NOTE

We've structured this book as a resource for leaders, offering guidelines, tips, and suggestions to use in the expanding virtual workplace. We've also provided additional checklists and resources in the appendices, along with summary guides in the last chapter for overcoming obstacles that leaders and team members may face.

Throughout the book, we have included many direct quotes from the people who shared their experiences through our surveys and interviews. Their comments are captured using the following graphic:

"These sidebars include quotes from leaders and team members we interviewed and surveyed. The focus of our research was on the challenges leaders and teams have faced and the solutions they've implemented to effectively navigate the path toward the *next normal.* Insights relate to success strategies for leading from a distance and managing remote and hybrid teams."

Collectively, we have over forty years of experience with remote teams, virtual leadership, and telework, along with decades of working with hundreds of client organizations across a broad array of industries. Through the years we've gathered a variety of personal experiences, from best practices to comical anecdotes. These experiences are called out in the chapters similar to the graphic below:

> **IN OUR EXPERIENCE...**
>
> *Building on our experience and the books we've previously published on related topics, we share our insights and learnings related to the topic at hand in these sections.*

Finally, we frequently highlight key takeaways, ideas, or important points using this graphic element:

> These are key points from the text that we think are worthy of a special highlight.

We hope that the following pages provide an abundance of information that helps remote leaders be more successful in supporting their team members who will increasingly comprise work-from-anywhere and hybrid teams.

On a related note, we thought you might want to know…

We've known each other for nearly ten years, enjoyed collaborating on the publication of this co-authored book (no easy feat under the best of co-located circumstances), and we've never had an in-person meeting!

We've both tried to "walk the talk" throughout the decades we've been involved in remote work. Through this book we look forward to showing you the way to accomplish this. May the path toward expanded remote work be as successful for you!

PREFACE

Our goal in writing this book is to provide leaders with the tools they need now and for the future as the virtual workplace evolves. With the likely increase of remote work as our "next normal," and in spite of its challenges, this is how and where the essential work of a growing number of organizations will get done. The challenges of building trust, communicating, collaborating, onboarding, coaching, motivating, problem solving, and maintaining organizational culture while leading work-from-anywhere and *hybrid* teams is the leadership imperative for the next era of remote work.

What are hybrid teams, and how will work-from-anywhere actually work? Work is shifting to where people are, rather than moving people to the physical workplace. While not all jobs can be accomplished remotely, we've seen that an increasing number of jobs can successfully be done from a distance. And there's increasing demand by workers to work from locations that are removed from the physical workplace—or even work from different locations at the preference of the individual worker. In many cases there's a blending of remote work with occasional work in the traditional workplace. For a number of reasons, the group of team members on-site at any particular time may vary, with an alternating mix of on-site and remote team members. This produces the hybrid team effect, where shifting groups of team members revolve through physical and distant forms of "presence."

What was previously an occasional, temporary, or limited aspect of the workplace, causing limited impact on leaders, is now a growing reality of organizational life for the future. Smart leaders will stay ahead of this curve, anticipate ways to adapt, and ensure they are prepared to meet the demands of leadership effectiveness in the new world of work, where teams must work well together from wherever they are and however they engage in teamwork.

We've both written on these topics, delivered related presentations and training, and been involved in helping leaders and organizations shift to remote work since the early days of telecommuting, when teleworkers typically only worked at home occasionally. Over the past two decades, the benefits of remote work have become clearer, and technology has advanced to meet the need for easier and more productive remote work. Intermittent weather, security, and infrastructure challenges, as well as growing awareness of the carbon footprint created by commuters, have all contributed to the growth in remote work and work-from-home initiatives. And then the global pandemic of 2020 hit, creating millions of "instant telecommuters" around the world.

As a result, the virtual workplace is no longer a trend; it's an inevitability that has become our new reality, creating new challenges and opportunities for leaders.

In recent years leaders have become more adept at leading from a distance, but the evolving dynamics of work create shifts in the on-site workplace and how leaders manage both on-site and remote team members. These dynamics restructure the workplace to include increasingly hybrid work teams. While it seemed challenging in the recent past to manage the occasional telecommuter, the random remote team member, or the one-off geo-dispersed team, hybrid teams add a layer of complexity to the mix. Fortunately, leaders can use fundamental leadership skills to lead hybrid teams effectively, with appropriate adaptation for these new workplace and work-team circumstances.

Leaders must now continually address the needs of team members who are sometimes remote, sometimes in the office, and rarely all together in one place. Leaders need to leverage "virtual presence" skills and build trust within dispersed teams; communicate without the benefit of in-person interaction; share information, collaborate, and innovate via digital tools; coach from a distance; hire and onboard remotely; inculcate cultural values virtually; and achieve performance targets in new ways.

> **"The biggest and most important ongoing challenges are building relationships and maintaining trust. You don't have an organization without good relationships, and trust."**

These skills are essential for the new era of leadership that is required in a wide range of organizations and in shifting circumstances. Understanding how to adapt leadership skills to effectively support remote team members and hybrid teams is essential for leaders now.

Leaders will also need to forge new territory relative to planning and policies for the growing work-from-anywhere segment of the workforce. Challenging as it's been to craft telework programs for a select few team members, leaders are now faced with greater complexity in designing flexible work arrangements to accommodate a variety of circumstances. This requires formulating policies regarding remote worker selection, performance management, career development, technology, safety, and equipment, as well as legal, compliance, and tax implications.

While the traditional workplace will still exist, how it works and how people interact within it has evolved. What is no longer debatable, however, is the permanent shift in response to both the demand and need for flexibility. We've already seen that the physical workplace, which may not be accessible to significant segments of the workforce, can no longer be the only place where meaningful work is accomplished. Aside from the talent acquisition and retention benefits for employers of a more flexible approach to work, legions of workers will expect expanded work-from-anywhere options in support of their desire to minimize commute time and improve work-life balance.

More critically, organizations can no longer be unprepared for the next weather, security, or national health emergency that renders the traditional workplace unusable. Rather, organizations, leaders, and teams must be prepared to continue their critical work—from wherever it can be done—to meet customer needs and market demand. And they must know how to do this well, with the right skills to lead and the necessary team effectiveness to continue delivering required results.

Debra A. Dinnocenzo
Pittsburgh, PA USA
January 2021

Jason Morwick
Orlando, FL USA
January 2021

INTRODUCTION

It's hard to believe that it's been almost fifty years since the term telecommuting was first coined. In an age before the Internet and mobile technology, and even before fax machines were widely used, early visionaries imagined a time when people could work from home. No longer would teams be constrained by boundaries of the office walls. Twenty years later, telecommuting gave way to remote work and the virtual workplace, as technology caught up and enabled those early ideas. Finally, it seemed, work-from-anywhere was a reality.

However, innovations in technology preceded advancements in organizational behavior. Although there were plenty of tools to untether employees from a specific location, many leaders were reluctant to allow team members to work out of sight. Many advocates of remote work believed that every year was the year that the virtual workplace would become the norm. Over the past decade, some organizations went through a cycle of formally implementing remote work, only to rein it back in as it expanded beyond the leaders' comfort zone. Some were ready to sound the death knell for remote work, but we noticed that something more interesting was happening. Remote work was far from over. In fact, it seemed that work was becoming more flexible, more mobile, and more distributed, while there were fewer formal remote working arrangements driven from corporate headquarters. Instead, informal, local arrangements were agreed upon between leaders and their team members. Working remotely, on a limited basis, seemed to become widely accepted.

Teams evolved well before the COVID-19 pandemic struck in early 2020, but the mandatory shutdowns and quarantines provided the proverbial tipping point for remote work. There was no choice but to send team members home and try to keep business going. Some organizations that already had experience with remote work found that a full transition into the remote environment went smoother than expected. Employees continued to get work done; leaders continued to lead their teams. Although the situation for most leaders wasn't ideal, many discovered how well they and their teams could perform while working remotely, and they could envision how the workplace might change after the pandemic was over.

In our research for this book, we surveyed and interviewed hundreds of leaders and team members during the COVID-19 pandemic from across industries in varying company sizes. In many cases, people discovered how to work remotely for the first time. When asked how often they worked remotely prior to the pandemic, 40% of the respondents answered, "Not at all." Yet, only about 7% wanted to go back to the office full time and never work remotely again. The vast majority responded with some combination of working in the office and working remotely. Just over 20% of survey participants who were already working remotely to some degree prior to the pandemic wanted to increase the amount of time away from the office when the pandemic was over. In short, people overwhelmingly want some degree of flexibility to work remotely (see Figure 1).

Remote Work/Leadership Survey

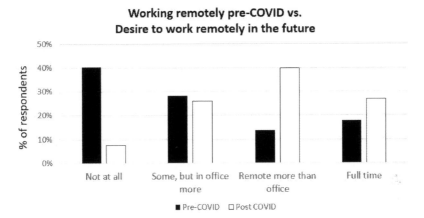

Working remotely pre-COVID vs. Desire to work remotely in the future

Source: Dinnocenzo/Morwick, 2020

Furthermore, what we found even more interesting is that there was no significant difference in desire to work remotely between leaders and team members. Studies done over a decade ago indicated that team members wanted to work remotely more than leaders. Presumably, many leaders were uncomfortable leading from a distance or untrusting of how their employees would perform if unsupervised. Our research led us to believe that leaders have evolved beyond that. When we asked what has gone well while working remotely, leaders were far more likely than team members to mention productivity, collaboration, and communication.

9

We have to point out that the size of the organization does appear to factor into a person's desire to work remotely. Smaller organizations, those with less than 1,000 employees, were more likely to have full-time remote workers than larger organizations, and larger organizations were more likely to have full-time office-bound workers. This may be due in part to differences in organizational culture or financial constraints (e.g., smaller organizations may be more inclined to encourage remote working with the objective to reduce real-estate costs). However, employees from large and small organizations alike have an almost equal desire for more remote work in the post-COVID-19 era.

TEAM MODELS

So where do we go from here? Workplaces will evolve into one of four team models. The first two models are familiar, but they will be increasingly uncommon in the future.

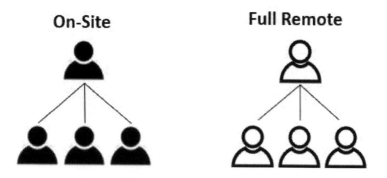

On-Site   **Full Remote**

The *On-Site* model is one we all know. It is the traditional office model where all employees are *co-located*—or located together at one site. This model also addresses when employees are co-located within different locations of the same organization. Leaders generally have direct line-of-sight to their team members. This model may be preferred in some cases based on the nature of work. For example, if employees handle sensitive information that cannot be accessed remotely or must do hands-on work such as manufacturing or construction, the on-site model will prevail. However, for knowledge-based work, it is unlikely that we will see continued use of this team model to the extent that it's been used in the past.

At the opposite end of the spectrum is the *Full Remote* model, where all work is done remotely and there is no actual co-located workspace. Start-ups and smaller companies may more readily choose this model to reduce operating expenses and real-estate cost. Automattic, the web development company behind the popular blog service WordPress.com, has fully embraced this concept with its 1,300 employees. However, we have yet to see large, Fortune 500 companies embrace the Full Remote model.

If the On-Site and Full Remote models will not be the norm, then what can we expect in the workplace of the very near future? Most organizations will leverage and transform into hybrid teams.

Hybrid Teams

Static Hybrid   **Fluid Hybrid**

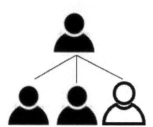
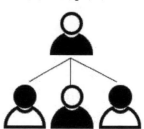

In our model of hybrid teams, the *Static Hybrid* team design has become common, though still an occasional, one-off, or special arrangement—often to accommodate the needs of a handful of team members. In this model, a critical mass of team members may be co-located on-site, while some individuals are permanently remote. Examples of this include sales organizations, with sales representatives working from home offices, and service organization, with service technicians located in the field closer to customers and often using home as their base of operation.

Face-to-face interactions with remote team members in the *Static Hybrid* model may be infrequent, if at all. This model benefits those with special needs or accommodates those with desired skills or talents that can't relocate to the company or team location.

Multinational and global companies may embrace the *Static Hybrid* model so they can strategically position teams or team members in countries where business is conducted. This model also describes organizations that take advantage of a wider national or global talent pool through distributed teams that are spread across geographic areas and time zones. Despite the fact that some members are co-located, everyone works remotely to some degree as they interact with off-site team members.

Most likely, *Fluid Hybrid* teams will be increasingly common in a growing number of organizations. The physical work location will still exist, but leaders and team members will have the flexibility to use the workplace as needed with remote work as the default mode. Organizations may benefit from higher employee satisfaction and engagement (and therefore higher retention) and reduction in overhead and real-estate costs.

As mentioned earlier, our survey of leaders and team members highlighted the desire to work remotely—*some of the time*. Approximately a quarter of respondents said they wanted to work remotely full-time, but two-thirds indicated they want to work remotely only part-time. Additionally, leaders cited the lack of personal interactions as the biggest challenge to working remotely. Team members identified this as one of their top challenges, while concerns about staying motivated and maintaining productivity ranked slightly higher. Most people are social creatures and want in-person, live human interaction. There will be a "sweet spot" for most employees—they will work in the office when necessary, but the balance of the time they'll work remotely.

Hybrid teams present many challenges and implications for leaders There may be shifting groups of team members that are present at different times; or a portion of the team might consistently work on-site with the leader, while others are primarily remote. These are some of the scenarios that are likely to create new challenges for remote leaders, requiring new skills and innovative approaches to working with teams. Therefore, leaders must prepare themselves to meet the needs of the new work environment and changing demands by their team members. In the chapters that follow, we discuss ways to meet the demands of these new working team models and how to achieve the best results for remote leaders and work-from-anywhere and hybrid teams.

1

BUILDING TRUST
IN THE
REMOTE WORKPLACE

We are living in a time when remote work is ramping up. Technology makes it easier for us to work together from a distance, but despite of our growing comfort with remote jobs, this kind of work arrangement still presents challenges. So much depends, of course, on how capable and reliable the myriad technology tools are. But the real concerns are more fundamental, rooted in our desire to truly connect with each other on a human level as we do our jobs.

How can people working remotely learn to rely on one another? How can they develop the crucial "sense" of knowing their coworkers and, more importantly, trusting them to understand, follow through, and be honest—in other words, be trustworthy?

This is both a difficult and critical challenge when team members are geographically separated, requiring leaders to build trust within remote and hybrid teams.

Trust is the underpinning of all effective relationships, and trust within remote teams is critical to the success of those teams and the organization. Developing trust in remote and hybrid teams is more challenging and is likely to take

> **"The main challenge still faced is building new relationships and trust with new individuals. This is what our business is built on."**

more time, patience, persistence, and creativity. However, the necessary level of trust within such teams can indeed be achieved.

Research on the development of trust has shown "that trust started lower in computer-mediated teams but increased to levels comparable to those in face-to-face teams over time. Furthermore, this pattern of results also held for teams that switched from face-to-face to electronic media and vice versa." (Wilson)

Remote leaders must now strike a balance between the fluctuating on-site presence of fluid hybrid team members interacting in variable groupings and the continual interactions of remote team members utilizing distance communication tools. Leaders might never have had to call upon such skills before or been expected to handle these challenges to the extent expected now. Fortunately, there are effective tools remote leaders can use to achieve success in leading dispersed teams.

TRUST BEGINS WITH AND BEGETS COMMUNICATION

The relationship between trust and communication is a strong one. To lead an increasingly dispersed workforce, leaders must have a commitment to both quality and frequency of communication. Without a strong basis of trust,

> **Both quality & frequency of communication are important.**

communication is compromised, confusion and conflict reign, motivation and collaboration decline, employee retention and satisfaction erode, and productivity suffers.

While trust within a team can be impacted by the culture of systemic or organizational trust, we'll focus here on the level of interpersonal trust that leaders more directly influence within their teams and in their relationships with individual team members.

> **"Communicating decisions and information to those who don't have the background knowledge can often lead to misunderstanding which leads to mistrust."**

We'll discuss communication in more depth in the following chapter, but here we'll highlight a few aspects of communication that particularly impact trust in remote teams.

THE POWER OF DISCLOSURE

Sharing information regarding organizational direction, employee expectations and changes that impact team objectives is an important aspect of communication and trust building. The most effective leaders are also aware of the power of disclosure.

What does it mean for a leader to use disclosure? Leaders disclose by sharing information, perspectives, personal insights, concerns, experiences, and feelings, along with expressing empathy that can positively impact trust and rapport. This is especially important when interpersonal dynamics between the leader and team members occur in the virtual environment. When a remote leader skillfully and appropriately uses disclosure, it humanizes the leader and provides a more authentic connection with team members. Connections like this build a foundation of trust within the team.

Use disclosure to build connection & trust.

Disclosure is a powerful tool because it conveys empathy, and leaders can use disclosure to strengthen rapport or show a commitment to action. Although some leaders may feel reluctant to show vulnerability by sharing personal experiences, challenges, or even failures, these types of disclosures can open doors of dialogue, an especially helpful technique when building trust from a distance.

"We continually ask for feedback, look for our people to assist us in how to manage this 'new normal', being transparent about what we know, when we know it, and also (this is key) what we don't know."

18

> **IN OUR EXPERIENCE...**
>
> *Throughout the COVID-19 pandemic that resulted in many difficult work-from-home scenarios, we heard team leaders use disclosure to demonstrate (and perhaps to seek) empathy during webinars, video meetings, online training, and teleconferences The challenges during this time were especially complicated by children at home when schools and childcare services were closed, resulting in discomfort by team members concerned about how others would perceive potential distractions and interruptions. When leaders had the opportunity, they put team members at ease, conveyed understanding, and used disclosure with comments such as: "My 4-year-old will probably drop by occasionally just to hug me." "You might hear my 15-month-old baby crying." "I have seven dogs and 3 cats – you may see some of them during the meeting." "If a package is delivered, my dog will go nuts and bark like crazy!"*

The disclosure should be relevant to the situation and should be a sincere reflection of actual experience or feelings the leader has lived, e.g., "Been there, done that."

Disclosure should not include sharing anything so personal that it makes team members uncomfortable or the disclosure is inappropriate, such as sexual pursuits or previous illegal behavior. The point of disclosure is to demonstrate empathy and to build bonds, allowing the leader to support team members in handling a difficult situation, overcoming an obstacle, or opening the door to a meaningful discussion.

In the remote work environment where connections can be harder to establish or maintain, leaders who convey greater openness and authenticity through disclosure can build strong bridges of trust.

BRIDGING DIFFERENCES

Other factors—such as generational, personality, and cultural differences—can affect the functioning and underlying trust within a dispersed team. It is important to recognize that generational differences can influence communication styles, technology preferences, and comfort levels with different communication methodologies. Leaders of multi-generational virtual and hybrid teams find that they need to calibrate the frequency and types of communication to the needs of individual team members. So, if a hybrid team is multi-generational, the leader needs to recognize this, discuss which technology tools team members prefer, and provide the tools that best support communication and collaboration among team members.

These situations create opportunities for leaders to seek input from team members, enabling the team to help shape the leader's approach and the way the team works together. Discussing generational differences as a challenge will open dialogue that leads to solutions built through team collaboration, resulting in greater commitment to the outcome and higher levels of empathy and trust within the team.

> Identify and problem solve generational & cultural differences.

Cultural differences among team members can also influence preferred communication methods and trust development. Leaders of multinational teams must be sensitive to cultural differences within their teams and how these differences affect team dynamics and interactions.

Take, for example, the challenges of team members in multiple time zones. We've seen situations where scheduled multinational team meeting times that are always biased to one time zone (usually where headquarters or the team leader is located). But scheduling every meeting for management convenience disenfranchises team members located on the other side of the globe, requiring them to participate in meetings during their non-work hours.

> **IN OUR EXPERIENCE...**
>
> *A leader for a global company had department members across several countries. Without realizing it, he scheduled a meeting on a day that was on a national holiday for a few team members. The team members in that country didn't feel comfortable raising an issue to the leader and attended the meeting. Months later, word got back to the leader that some team members let it be known that it was a little insensitive.*

Remote team leaders of global or intercultural teams might also bump into other obstacles associated with cultural differences, including language barriers, national holiday schedules, local customs relative to work hours, and personal preferences that impact behavior involving communication and collaboration. How should a remote team leader handle so many different variables within a team?

While there are no boilerplate answers that apply in all situations, leaders should start with awareness, empathy, and openness to finding solutions that meet the needs of team members. Begin by asking the team for suggestions. Working with the team to overcome obstacles rooted in cultural differences will help the team become a successful, culturally integrated virtual team.

KEYS TO TRUST

The key elements of trust are familiarity, reliability, and integrity. All three are especially challenging when team members are dispersed. It's even harder to build trust when fluid hybrid teams create a less stable, more dynamic, ever changing workplace environment and work team presence. This results in team members who are less familiar with each other. For this kind of team, learning to rely on each other and be assured of each member's integrity becomes more complex.

> "Workflow and communication were problems for us. We overcame them by letting go of micro-managing and trusting the team."

But experience has shown that trust can be created and maintained when leaders are mindful of how trust is established and the ways to nurture it. Building trust within virtual and hybrid teams begins with familiarity.

FAMILIARITY

Familiarity develops in traditional workplaces as people work alongside each other, learning not only how to work together but—more critically—learning about each other as people. In the normal course of working together on-site, team members get to know each other on a personal level beyond the workplace. This typically includes sharing information about family, friends, hobbies, interests, and the like. Why is this important? It creates the sense of really knowing each other, and it's a vital part of building trusting relationships.

Beyond just getting along well at work, team members and leaders need to have a sincere interest each other's non-work lives, concerns, and challenge. An effective way to demonstrate this in distant teams is to follow-up on details learned about individual team members. During team or individual check-in discussions, remember to ask about situations that a team member has previously discussed with colleagues or shared with the team leader.

Make time for small talk & getting to know team members.

This is especially true when a team member is struggling with family concerns, health issues, or distance work challenges. Continued follow-up by the leader, as well as the offer of support when possible, ensures that team members feel heard and valued, which helps build trust.

Personal Connections Support Familiarity

Digital communication tends to be more focused on the task at hand. The information exchanges that happen when team members work together on-site or meet face-to-face often don't naturally occur during virtual meetings. Remote leaders need to be aware of the need and encourage the kind of communication that builds familiarity from a distance. Leaders can support this by structuring virtual meeting agendas that include time for informal or personal sharing among team members. Consider scheduling calls or meetings that are focused only on personal interactions by hosting virtual coffee break, happy hour, or shared lunch hour.

As remote teams work together over a longer time, they naturally develop more comfort with the kind of virtual interactions that support strong personal bonds. So why aren't all virtual leaders nurturing familiarity in this way? Many complain about the demands on their time and having "too much on our plates."

These are valid concerns. We're hard-pressed to think of any leaders we know who are not doing more with less now and feeling time crunched every day. But if leaders consider the alternative—and how productivity would be affected if trust within their team was compromised—leaders quickly recognize the value of investing time in building trust. When we have presented this concept to leaders...the lightbulbs start lighting up!

IN OUR EXPERIENCE...

A maintenance team leader of a power utility company revamped his daily update meetings with supervisors and managers during the 2020 pandemic to facilitate deeper familiarity within his team. The team leader designated that 3 of 5 daily meetings each week would be restricted to NO discussions related to work. This provided the opportunity and the time for discussion related only to the concerns, well-being, challenges, and 'good news' that team members shared with each other. This also encouraged a 'trickle-down' of this mindset, as his supervisors and managers applied the no-work-topics mandate in some of their team meetings.

Debra, one of the authors, was engaged in a distant work relationship with a video distributor based in another region of the country. The power of familiarity proved critical. They collaborated throughout the various phases of the project—from production to material development to video marketing strategy to sales support—over several years to grow video revenues and provide client implementation support. The relationship became mutually dependent and advantageous, and they developed a rapport as well as trust in each other.

Debra and the distributor came to really like and respect each other and enjoyed talking about their lives, interests, and challenges—within the context of a productive, professional relationship focused on results. Developing the personal side of this relationship took more time, of course, than sticking to a task-limited focus during our virtual meetings, but it also offered many benefits. While they never met (and haven't to this day), this relationship is a positive model of building trust through familiarity, even from a distance.

Familiarity among co-workers occurs more naturally when team members work side-by-side and requires less attention by leaders in the traditional workplace. However, awareness and development of familiarity for distance teams requires a more focused effort by leaders to ensure that trust develops as a positive dynamic within the team.

Replicate & simulate the on-site work experience.

Remote leaders must continually and creatively take steps to *replicate* the ways co-located team members develop familiarity and *simulate* those activities, actions, techniques, and interactions in the digital communication environment in which their teams function. And it doesn't always have to be about work— teams naturally want and need to have connections beyond formal work matters.

Informal Connections Are Important

To support development of team familiarity, leaders can integrate non-work discussion opportunities, virtual team development activities, and FUN events into virtual interactions. If the team had previously gathered for the occasional pizza party, schedule a "virtual pizza" event. For an ice cream social, send ice cream gift cards in advance of a scheduled virtual ice cream event. Or schedule "lunch & learn" opportunities for presentations or discussions on topics not directly related to work.

Coming up short on ideas? Ask if any team members want to take a turn leading these events by sharing a topic of particular interest to them that is unrelated to their job duties. The possibilities are endless—it just requires out-of-the-box thinking and leveraging the interests and talents of team members.

Manage Virtual Meetings To Build Familiarity

Leaders of global teams face unique challenges in building familiarity among team members because of infrequent face-to-face interactions and a variety of differences within the team. For these teams, it's important to manage and adapt digital interactions in ways that encourage rather than complicate nurturing familiarity when team members are remote. It's also necessary to avoid remote team members having a lesser role in team meetings or missing some elements of the team gathering.

Using effective remote meetings guidelines (see Chapter 3) can make virtual meetings both more productive and more supportive of building familiarity within the team. For example, rotating the meeting or discussion leader role among dispersed team members creates opportunities for team members to participate in more engaging and visible ways.

IN OUR EXPERIENCE...

One of the teams we've worked with implemented their own 'get more acquainted' activity when a team leader invited colleagues to join him for "Cooking with Winston" sessions. Menu ingredients were shared in advance, and everyone cooked the meal in their own kitchen while the team collectively followed Winston's instructions via videoconference. The first meal the team prepared was a chicken dish — made more memorable by one team member who introduced the team to his pet chicken! (No — this chicken was NOT used for the meal!)

As teams become increasingly virtual with few, if any, team members co-located for team meetings, team leaders are more likely to distribute meeting materials in advance or make meeting information available in ways that are easily accessible to distant team members.

IN OUR EXPERIENCE...

When the global help desk team of a multinational bank analyzed their functioning as a geo-dispersed team, several key insights guided their improvement steps. Remote team members shared that they felt at a disadvantage because team members based at USA headquarters, along with the senior VP leading the team, were able to meet face-to-face during team meetings, while individual remote members were never able to 'sit at the table' with their leader. The solution was to switch weekly team meets to 'all virtual.' This provided a more level playing field, as all team members engaged from their computers and none sat with the team leader.

Build A Remote-First Culture

As remote and hybrid teams more typically use digital tools to interact, collaborate, share information, and hold team meetings, a *remote-first* culture will evolve. To shift the organizational culture toward remote-first, leaders of dispersed and fluid hybrid teams continually find ways to strengthen their use of digital communication tools to build trust within teams and help remote team members feel more included.

> Encourage a "remote-first" culture.

With a remote-first approach, remote team members no longer feel isolated or have the sense of being an afterthought in the way information is shared. Shifting to a remote-first culture—rather than remote being the less common (and less supported) way of working—will establish remote work as the primary way of working, or at least on a par with the traditional on-site work environment.

The Impact Of Communication On Trust Building

When leaders model familiarity for team members, they are showing the way toward more familiarity amongst team members, as well as building familiarity between themselves and their teams. But familiarity requires communication.

As our workplace becomes more dispersed and team members are more distant from each other, effective remote leaders recognize that this is NOT the time to under-communicate. Have more frequent touch points. Multiple short weekly check-ins are better than one long discussion every other week. Frequent contact enhances the sense of connection that is essential to building familiarity and trust.

This is NOT the time to under-communicate.

Creating opportunities and making time for familiarity-building discussions during remote and hybrid team interactions replaces some of what team members miss by not being co-located. "Being remote means that we won't bump into each other in the hall or get to know someone from another team while grabbing a cup of coffee. We need to intentionally create interactions within our team so that we can all get to know each other." (Griffis)

"Daily (virtual) huddle is now part of the culture.

Using all the technology tools available, including those that allow for visual connections as well as voice-only calls, allow leaders to make the connection 'live' rather than utilizing less personal, non-synchronous connections—such as text and email. It's also best to use a mix of communication types to vary touchpoints with team members. Every effort to connect with team members doesn't have to be a formal, structured, or lengthy event. Remote leaders can strengthen familiarity with and among team members in many ways.

Informal, impromptu check-ins

Make it a point to reach out frequently to team members for video, or at least voice, calls to gauge how the team member is doing, mentally and emotionally. During these 'How goes it?' calls, ask questions and to offer help. If necessary, schedule these calls in advance to avoid missed connections.

Use the calls to show interest in the team member's life. Inquire about family, personal interests outside of work, or personal challenges. This will help the leader to better understand other factors that might impact the performance of team members.

Leverage existing meetings or events

The easiest way to discuss non-work topics might be to incorporate it into a previously scheduled or recurring meeting. The leader can set aside time in a team staff meeting or individual update meeting to discuss non-work topics. Team members can share personal news, discuss how they are currently feeling, or explain how they are handling challenges.

Create team events to increase rapport

Schedule virtual team lunches, coffee breaks, or happy hours. Create opportunities for fun and rapport-building, such as book or movie reviews, family highlights, pet introductions, or cooking together events. Encourage team members to host home office (or digital nomad location) tours. Celebrate birthdays, company service anniversaries, work successes, and other personal happy events such as births, weddings, special milestone anniversaries, or graduations. Alternatively, leaders can host virtual game sessions, with friendly competition where possible. And yes, leaders should try to get team members to meet in-person occasionally if feasible.

Create team learning events

> Develop a "You can count on me" team culture.

Leaders can schedule team learning events or supplement online individual learning with team reviews or debrief discussions. Discussion can include topics relevant to the business or industry developments. On a more personal level, team members can be tasked with learning an interesting bit of trivia about other team members. Keep in mind that not all of this has to be done in a meeting or even live. Learning and information sharing can be done using asynchronous tools—such as a knowledge bases, team intranet, social media, or a myriad of Cloud-based resources available.

RELIABILITY

People with shared objectives, accountabilities, or outcomes need to be able to depend on each other to follow through on commitments. The team, as a whole, needs to commit to reliability. This key component of trust development takes on particular importance as teams become geographically dispersed and face-to-face interactions are increasingly rare.

Leaders of virtual and hybrid teams must ensure reliability between team members—and, of course, be reliable themselves in their interactions with team members. When teams are co-located, co-workers can interact more directly to obtain information, seek clarification, and follow-up in more personal ways. But without these benefits of the traditional workplace, the need for reliability among team members becomes more critical in avoiding erosion of trust, particularly as hybrid teams become more fluid. There are several ways leaders can model reliability and ensure team members can count on each other.

Find the right people and provide them the right tools

Leaders should be mindful of selecting team members who demonstrate and embrace reliability as one of their core competencies (see Chapter 4 for more information on hiring and onboarding). Additionally, leaders must ensure that team members have reliable tools, technology, and information resources to deliver results reliably.

Focus on the little things—they can make a big difference

Reliability is a habit that can be demonstrated daily. For example, leaders should participate in scheduled meetings and begin them on time, respond to messages or requests promptly (or at least communicate a definite time when a response should be expected), and conduct regular check-ins with remote team members. Leaders should also follow through on commitments, honor agreements, meet deadlines, and be prompt when offering praise or feedback for improving performance.

Make reliability a priority

If the importance of reliability is discussed during team meetings and reliable behavior is agreed upon as a team value, then the team is much more likely to embrace it and act accordingly.

To reinforce desired behaviors, team members who demonstrate reliability should be recognized and the leader can link specific examples of how the associate positively impacted other team members, the organization, or other collaborators.

Be transparent

Reliability and honesty or openness often go hand-in-hand. When changes are introduced or expectations shift, leaders should share as much information as possible as early as possible. This will strengthen trust within the team.

Leaders should also seek input on how they can be more responsive to the needs of their team members and ask team members to identify ways they can be more responsive to each other.

INTEGRITY

Integrity is another critical element of building trust within teams. "Leadership integrity is vital to maintaining trust within your team. Integrity reflects how people perceive your honesty and the degree to which you respect the rights of others." (Dinnocenzo) When a leader lacks integrity or team members feel the leader's integrity can be compromised, the team lacks a reliable leader. Other elements of trust cannot overcome the negative consequences of failed integrity. Therefore, it is not an overstatement to suggest that it's vital that leaders act with integrity in every situation and ensure the integrity of their teams.

Team members who work remotely can experience confusion, and misunderstandings happen. They can develop damaging perceptions that are not easily identified or remedied from a distance. That's why frequent communication is so vital. Knowing when perception is shifting gives the leader the chance to straighten out any misunderstandings.

Leaders who increasingly manage a fluid mix of on- and off-site team members must be constantly vigilant of how information is distributed, the timing of information flow, and the content of information, as

> Nurture and require honesty, transparency, and respect.

well as how that information is received and perceived. Global teams, different cultures, variable time zones, and limited face-to-face communication opportunities will present challenges. To overcome these challenges, leaders must not only communicate often, but they must also communicate with transparency, honesty, and respectfulness. Integrity can be demonstrated and reinforced in day-to-day team interactions.

Make a commitment

It almost seems unnecessary to say, but everyone should commit to honesty in all communication, interactions, and actions. Leaders can discuss the importance of integrity within the team and assert integrity as a clear expectation and team value. This should coincide with organizational policies and cultural values that stress ethical behavior.

Walk the Talk

Actions always speak louder than words. Leaders can demonstrate their commitment to integrity by providing forthright, honest, fair, and balanced feedback to team members. Second, leaders should maintain confidences and handle sensitive information appropriately. Furthermore, prompt action to address matters of dishonesty and removing team members who violate ethical or moral standards will also ensure integrity is upheld within the team.

Team meetings can be used to seek questions or concerns regarding matters of integrity within the team and initiate discussion on issues that are creating rumors or distrust within the team. Discussion can be initiated to address any issues that are creating rumors or distrust within the team. Lastly, leaders and team members should avoid sarcasm, joking, and teasing in distance interactions that can be offensive or misinterpreted.

Trust is part of the foundation of successful remote leadership, but it's not the only part. In the following chapters, we'll explore communication, culture, talent acquisition and development, and other leadership skills needed as the nature of the workplace evolves.

But as teams become more dispersed, communication is more technology-dependent, and more work is done from a distance, trust is vital. Successful remote leaders will master the approaches, tools, and techniques to effectively lead remotely with a strong base of trust.

2

COMMUNICATING FROM A DISTANCE

Communicating from a distance can be difficult! In the aftermath of the "instant virtual workplace" created by the COVID-19 pandemic, which led to lockdowns in early 2020, many leaders learned this the hard way. But why is it so challenging?

When we asked a wide range of leaders and team members about the challenges they faced in communicating with each other, they reported problems associated with:

- Impromptu interactions
- Informal conversations
- Non-verbal cues
- Misunderstandings
- Isolation
- Sharing ideas
- Digital overload
- Collective thinking/problem solving

> "You miss the subtle cues on how someone is doing by not seeing them on a regular basis."

- Relationship building
- Water-cooler collaboration
- Sense of real human connection
- Video meeting fatigue

As Adam Goodheart points out, "Connectivity is not the same thing as connection." (USA Today, July 26, 2000). What's different today, however, is that we now have vastly expanded capabilities of digital communication—and yet we still struggle with how to leverage those forms of connectivity in ways that meet our needs and expectations for meaningful connection. The path to the level of connection we want begins with effective communication.

"It's easy for relationships to get frayed due to misunderstandings."

Clear communication is the foundation for many of the other remote-work success keys we will discuss throughout this book. Think about it: Can you build trust, hire effective team members, or solve problems without sound communication? Of course not. Remote leaders must find practical solutions to the challenges of *distance dialogue*. This means mastering the technology tools available to communicate effectively and lead people at a distance.

Distance Dialogue Challenges & Opportunities

By 2020, many organizations had carefully built communication protocols, established a technology infrastructure, and chosen a remote-first culture to support effective communication for remote teams. But many more had not, and their shortcomings in these critical components became painfully clear when the pandemic hit. These companies were forced to figure out new ways to conduct business remotely "on the fly."

Consider, for example, the impact of the pandemic on the expansion of telemedicine; downturns in travel and hospitality; and the legions of customer service agents who became instant teleworkers. Some organizations pivoted with relative ease; but many others were caught without a plan. It's clear to everyone now that remote work will expand, and hybrid teams will increasingly be the norm as we move past the pandemic. Wise leaders will be prepared for this next normal.

In retrospect, you can see that we had been moving toward remote work since the 1980s. It's difficult to identify many organizations that remain untouched by digital commerce and remote communication. Almost every business now uses voicemail, email, personal computers, ethernet, Internet, hand-held devices, search engines, and social media. Technology has altered how we work and how information reaches our homes, as well as the intersection between work and home. Many people were already working from home before the pandemic, and many more wish to have that opportunity; there's been a notable increase in the number of workers who would even take a cut in pay for the option to work remotely!

At the same time, the norm was for a company to be based in a physical workplace. They might have shifted between fixed-wall offices, cubicles, and open office spaces, but the traditional, in-person office was always there. Having most of the workers on-site met multiple needs; it helped prove that work was being done effectively, it fostered a sense of community, and it gave employees experience in teamwork—including effective communication. But the days of being in our communication comfort zones, with primarily face-to-face interactions and on-site meetings, are gone. They won't be as prevalent in the future, for a number of reasons.

Business leaders have found that catastrophes—like weather emergencies, power outages, major road closures, fires, floods, national security threats, public health concerns—are easier to manage if workers are prepared to use technology to stay connected and to provide business continuity without dependence on access to the physical workplace.

> **Remote work is expanding due to both demand and necessity.**

After the pandemic hit, millions of workers and leaders suddenly faced the challenges of working from home and working together from a distance. And now that they've proven remote work is both possible and effective, it's likely more employees will want this option into the future, at least a few days each week. They want to minimize commuting time and maximize the flexibility of where they can live.

Leaders also are calculating the costs of empty real estate and savings in travel expense, while considering the potential for new work models that benefit the organization, its customers, its people, their families, and our communities.

It's likely that the confluence of these realities will escalate the demand for remote work. We all need to be ready to increasingly work and communicate from a distance— and to manage the increased presence of remote and hybrid teams. How can leaders do this well?

It Starts (Like Everything) With Culture

Every organization and team has a distinct culture that influences the behaviors and perceptions of associates (see more on organizational culture in Chapter 6). The communication protocols and guidelines a leader develops within a team will be, ideally, consistent with the organization's overall culture. The

"Establishing communication guidelines helped."

way remote employees are managed also will be affected by the organization's culture. The organization might want to establish a remote-first environment or simply embrace distance team members as occasional but valued members of the organization.

43

> **Clarify needs and implement digital communication standards.**

Either way, establishing the proper digital communication standards or protocols begins with "raising awareness and increasing sensitivity to the communication needs of everyone on the team—and ensuring that all team members understand the impact on their communication methods and techniques." (Dinnocenzo)

If the organization's digital communication methods evolved in a haphazard way, or cultural barriers exist, technology resources might be ill-suited to the team's needs. Clear communication standards and expectations might not have been clarified. This is certainly true when remote work is implemented on an emergency basis, after a disaster. A business without all these elements in place might see productivity shortfalls, decline in responsiveness to customers, and vast amounts of frustration all around.

As business consultants, we know that top-level sponsorship or support is the best way to implement programs and processes. But that's not always the kind of support an organization gets. The organization's digital communication protocols might not be established on an organization-wide level. They might not even be consistent with overall organizational strategy and values.

What can be done in this case? No worries—leaders of divisions, groups, departments, or teams can work within their own teams to establish the standards, expectations, and protocols. Leaders can identify the tools their teams need to smoothly implement remote work and distance dialogue. You simply have to start where you are. First, consider cultural influences, assess the current state, identify opportunities and obstacles so you can establish clear digital communication standards.

A tool to help leaders get started is the Digital Communication Assessment found in Appendix C. Once the current digital communication environment is clearly understood, leaders can work with their teams to reach agreements on needed guidelines and resources for remote communication. It's likely that this process will ultimately involve collaboration with other internal groups, such as the information technology department, finance, and human resources. They'll need to be aware of any needs or changes in the team, and they should be able to provide training and development options or other resources.

The Distance Difference

Leaders and team members seem to agree on the advantages of face-to-face interactions. Such communication is considered better, easier, and more productive. Face-to-face meetings lead to more natural collaboration, right?

Of course, it's also true that organizational life is easier when everyone agrees, customers submit unsolicited orders, and equipment never fails. But since we can't subscribe to the school of magical thinking—and we find

> **"If something happens or I perceive my team is down, I give them a call, or we chat. Sometimes we have longer talks, just to minimize the stress from being isolated."**

ourselves in a rapidly evolving surge of remote work—we need to focus on solutions that overcome the inevitable obstacles to communicating from a distance, and even recognize the benefits of remote leadership.

Distance dialogue is definitely different than in-person dialogue. If productivity and true collaboration are being compromised, it's not just because of the technical challenges and concerns; it's because using technology to communicate is not what we're used to. We humans are social beings, which is why social media is so popular. But even the most avid social media enthusiast will find that comfort with these resources doesn't

> **"It's harder to read people online. In-person, I can take in their body language, where they sit, if they look comfortable or bored."**

necessarily translate to comfort using distance communication in work settings. Why is that?

In reality, social media applications are increasingly used for supplementing business communication—but the typical business communication tools for distance dialogue continue to feel inferior to the ease with which teams interact when working together in the same physical space. Leaders need to find the best ways to use distance communication tools to replicate the in-person experience and simulate the ways interaction, communication, collaboration, and problem-solving occur in the physical workplace.

There's little value in saying "in-person is better" when a pandemic or some other emergency prevents us from meeting in-person. At some point, reality whacks us on the head, and it's more useful to focus on what we can do in this new situation and what advantages it might offer.

Virtual team members are always at risk of feeling and being marginalized. People tend to focus on those who are physically present rather than those sitting in cyberspace. As the workplace evolves to a more remote-first culture, this will become less of an obstacle. But even when all team members are virtual, the vocal minority can occupy more "air-time" and get more attention. The downside for those introverted, quieter, or culturally diverse virtual team members is that they might become less engaged over time. It's important to be mindful of these risks and take steps to encourage and enable (through coaching and training) all team members to engage in distance dialogue using the techniques that follow.

> **Keep remote team members visible and engaged.**

Planning

Make it a team habit to spend at least 5 minutes (or longer if presenting part of the agenda) preparing for upcoming team meetings. Block time on schedules if necessary. To help team members best prepare for meetings or discussions, having an agenda distributed in advance – or at least a statement of

> **"Sharing documents was problematic until we fully appreciated the need to provide them ahead of time."**

purpose & importance – provides meeting participants with the opportunity to prepare effectively.

Encouraging everyone to participate

Rotating roles and responsibilities for team meetings is a good way to get people involved. Assign someone to manage time, another to track the agenda, someone else to capture follow-up actions. Seek a volunteer to summarize each topic and/or the action steps.

The meeting leader is responsible for—as much as possible, depending upon the purpose and content of the meeting—encouraging participation from everyone by providing time to ask questions or asking for input. Don't dominate the conversation or feel the need to fill dead air. When virtual meeting participants are quiet, they may be disengaged or multitasking or uncomfortable being assertive in the virtual environment. Reach out to ask for input, ask by name for suggestions or questions, and verify understanding by summarizing periodically and making questioners feel welcome.

> **Encourage active meeting participation by everyone.**

As time passes and more meetings of remote and hybrid teams shift to video-based tools, team members will become more comfortable engaging online. But people can still be quiet, distracted, or confused during a video meeting. It's the leader's responsibility to involve everyone and proactively seek their engagement to ensure that everyone is on the same page and feels included.

Using video as the norm

Whenever possible, use video technology and set an expectation that webcams are on for everyone. Leaders are often concerned about their remote team members' productivity, accessibility, and engagement. Seeing each other via video can help circumvent these roadblocks. Here's why:

- **Confirming engagement.** Some managers simply do not trust that workers will use their time productively outside of a traditional office. This is *less* of an employee issue and *more* of a management issue. There's no evidence that workers are more responsible when they're on video. But being able to see them may give some managers a stronger sense of team member engagement, easing fears that employees are not focused on their work.

- **Nonverbal cues.** This one is the most frequently cited benefits of video-based communication. Without video, nonverbal cues such as body language and facial expressions are missing. This can result in misunderstandings, confusion, and inability to detect resistance. Some studies have focused on identifying the amount of information that's sent and received via body language compared to verbal communication. These studies show that people typically understand and retain *four times* as much information when communication includes a visual component rather than relying on verbal communication alone.

- **Meeting efficiency.** Being able to communicate visually makes meetings more efficient. When participants can observe visual cues, they can adjust their communication styles as necessary. They can avoid talking over each other, because it's easier to see when there's an opportunity to talk. This allows teams to be more effective in accomplishing meeting objectives.

- **Increasing interaction.** Virtual participants on a teleconference call are more inclined to multitask. There is an understandable tendency for participants to use their computer or phone while on 'mute' during a teleconference. But multitasking makes remote team members less focused on the meeting's goals. Video is much closer to in-person communication in holding the attention of meeting participants.

VIRTUAL ICEBREAKERS FOR VIRTUAL TEAMS

Icebreakers are quick, facilitated activities to help a team develop stronger rapport. There are a variety of exercises to choose from here, including activities directly related to the project at hand; more personal sharing; and even icebreakers that are a little zany, such as asking participants which photo of an animal best represents their mood at that moment. The exercises are an easy, fun, and fast way to help people get to know each other and overcome any hesitancy to participate. These team-building exercises also can help people build relationships more quickly, begin to build trust, and ultimately accelerate team cohesion and productivity.

IN OUR EXPERIENCE...

When a two-day leadership training program conducted online needed a little jolt of energy and motivation for more engagement, we created a quick "Leader Bingo" challenge. Using words we were likely to say throughout the remainder of the training, we created the virtual Bingo card, posted it in the shared documents section of the online tool, and (of course) announced the prize for the first participant to call "Bingo!" (Yes, these were grown adults, seasoned leaders, and highly motivated Bingo players!)

Variations on icebreakers can also be used to keep a longer virtual meeting more engaging. Use exercises like these to 'mix it up' when the team needs a break from the meeting agenda, or it seems like it's time to get everyone refocused on the meeting.

Icebreakers are common when people meet face-to-face, but we're seeing more application of these tools for virtual teams. Many of the commonly used icebreakers for face-to-face meetings can be used, with a little adaption, for virtual teams.

See Appendix A for examples of icebreakers for virtual team meetings.

CREATING A SENSE OF BEING TOGETHER

The essential challenge of communicating from a distance is creating a sense of *real* presence through *virtual* technologies. While technology can help bridge the distance to create technical connectivity, i.e., a web video link, it can also create barriers to the real types of connection we want to have with the people we work with, need to rely on, and with whom we want to have trusting relationships.

When people are actively engaged with each other, they are being *present* in their interactions. When we interact with each other remotely, we are creating *virtual presence*. Virtual presence is created by how technology tools are used and the impact this has on people's perceptions of each other. In a virtual meeting setting, it also refers to the perceived connections among participants.

Don't confuse this virtual presence with the way the term is used in other technologies, where it refers to "the ability of a user to feel that they are *actually in* a virtual location, such as a web site or an immersive simulation using technologies like virtual reality (VR) or augmented reality (AR)." (TechTarget) Meeting participants will always know they're not actually in the same room. But both types of virtual presence include the synchronous dynamic that creates the sense of "being there" with others.

So, how does this happen and what steps can leaders take to both model and nurture a greater degree of virtual presence for remote and hybrid teams?

As we have mentioned, the best way to achieve virtual presence is to focus on ways to simulate and replicate the things team members do and the ways they do them when they are working together face-to-face. Members of hybrid teams will, of course, most likely experience occasional on-site interactions—but increasingly this will happen with some team members working from a distance.

> **Leverage tech tools to create virtual presence to simulate real presence.**

This means that teams need to leverage technology resources and utilize these resources in ways that make the hybrid experience both seamless and as transparent as possible. This results in a shared hybrid experience for all team members, making physical presence an irrelevant factor.

It's vital that all team members have the same experience—they all see what's going on, hear at the same level, and detect the behavioral cues that contribute to the sense of real *presence*. Let's look at some of the critical ways to achieve a stronger virtual presence for the leader and the team, as well as the best ways to avoid pitfalls that erode virtual presence.

DYNAMICS THAT AFFECT VIRTUAL PRESENCE

Technology enables virtual connections. But understanding how to best lead and participate in virtual meetings will contribute significantly to a greater sense of virtual presence. Increasingly, virtual meetings incorporate video, which enhances virtual presence. Seeing other meeting participants makes for a more engaging experience. However, some team members might still be uncomfortable 'being on camera' and operating their technology tools.

> "We have become very proficient at virtual meetings and accomplish more in less time than we did with in-person meetings."

Here are some ways to use virtual meeting tools to minimize discomfort and enhance virtual presence. Use these to improve hybrid meetings—where some team members are on-site together, while others are remote. Some of these suggestions are applicable to teleconference meetings even when cameras are not in use.

❖ **Alternate eye contact between on-site participants and the camera(s)**

While it's natural and tempting to look at the other people sitting in the same room, focusing only on them creates an obstacle for hybrid teams and can make remote participants feel a sense of greater distance or even alienation. It requires a conscious effort to look at both on-site team members and the camera, to ensure that remote team members feel included—everyone makes that effort, there's a stronger sense of presence within the meeting.

❖ **Maintain a clear, strong voice, confirming that remote participants can hear**

It's easy to speak loudly enough for those in the room to hear, but that might not be sufficient for remote attendees. Resist the feeling of SHOUTING that might be created by speaking loudly and clearly enough for remote participants to hear comfortably. Check on sound levels with those joining remotely to ensure that there are no audio barriers that impact meeting effectiveness.

❖ **Avoid side comments among co-located participants**

Few things are more off-putting to remote meeting participants than the side banter than goes on between on-site participants. In the spirit of ensuring that everyone is having the same experience, save private remarks for after the meeting.

❖ **Direct comments, questions, and opportunities for input to both on-site and remote attendees**

Be sure that all discussion involves everyone participating in the meeting.

We've all participated in meetings from a distance that were led by people who seemed to forget that remote participants have joined the meeting. The increased use of video meetings is minimizing this problem, but it's important to always ensure that off-site meeting attendees are made to feel that they are 'there' with everyone else.

❖ **Be certain that the meeting leader and all on-site participants can be heard and seen by remote participants; likewise, ensure that everyone who is on- site can see/hear each remote team member**

Depending on the technology options available, this can be easy or challenging. As virtual meeting technology improves and competence with video meetings strengthens, this becomes less of a problem. And certainly, the pandemic of 2020 produced a vast amount of hands-on training in effective video meeting skills!

One solution is making everyone "remote." Many on-site groups disperse to individual locations and avoid gathering together in a meeting room. While this creates a greater number of individual remote connections, it creates the sense of a "level playing field" so that all participants can clearly see and hear each other.

❖ **Ensure that camera framing is set to be clear and focuses on the face, so that eyes and facial expressions can be seen by all meeting participants**

Again, the objective is to simulate being together for a meeting, where seeing the faces and visual cues of meeting participants is inherent. If a team member doesn't turn on their camera, has the camera pointed at their forehead, is out of focus, or is dimly lit, it compromises that participant's virtual presence.

Enhanced videoconference rooms are increasingly important as more remote and hybrid teams must meet. Without this level of technology, take care to manage this in a meeting room with on-site participants, particularly if only one camera is used

> **IN OUR EXPERIENCE...**
>
> *Video "presence" should be effective enough to observe a question or concern. During a recent video-based training session, it was clear that something was terribly concerning to a participant in Mexico. When we inquired (based on the worried look and anxious glances that were easily visible), we learned that an earthquake was underway!*

❖ **Ensure lighting is appropriate so you can clearly be seen without it being a distraction**

Even if a meeting participant can see other participants clearly, that doesn't mean all the other meeting attendees can see that participant. Good lighting is important and often overlooked. Effective lighting ensures that meeting participants can read facial expressions and nonverbal cues. Also, remember that too much lighting, such as a bright lamp in close view of the camera or sunlight streaming through a window can be distracting. Diffused daylight is usually ideal. And facing an artificial light source is preferrable.

❖ **Ensure there's a non-distracting background or use digital effects that help to focus attention on the participant.**

As videoconferencing tools become more user friendly and incorporate enhanced capabilities, resources are available that make this easier to accomplish. Since not everyone has an appropriate background or a portable backdrop for video meetings, using the digital effects embedded in virtual meeting tools is an effective solution. Leaders should ensure that all team members understand how to effectively use their video meeting tools. Virtual backgrounds are also helpful in protecting team member privacy for anyone who prefers not to have views of their home environment visible.

❖ **Ensure team members are wearing appropriate attire according to team norms**

Teleconferences provide more flexibility for super casual/comfortable dress for remote workers. Video meetings may require a more professional appearance. But, if the company culture is very casual, leaders may not care.

IN OUR EXPERIENCE...

One manager told us about a former employee. "He liked to wear t-shirts he found comical. One of the shirts said something like, "Show me the candy before I get in the van." Some people may have thought it was funny, but others found it inappropriate. However, I didn't say anything to him because he was working from home. I didn't think I could tell someone what they could wear in their own house."

Whatever the expectations are regarding dress standards, they should be clearly communicated. If some team members are co-located in an office and required to wear business casual attire, does that also apply to remote team members? Leaders need to set team norms and determine what is or is not appropriate when team members are on video. It's also important that norms and expectations be clarified for external meetings with customers or other collaborators.

> **IN OUR EXPERIENCE...**
>
> *An executive who was joining team meetings from home had a nice, paneled wall behind him...on which was mounted a HUGE GUN! Though not intentional, perhaps the symbolic (and potentially threatening) nature of that image led to a change in background before too long.*

❖ Stay engaged and focused throughout the meeting

While it's tempting to do other things during pauses or long explanations in virtual meetings, virtual meeting participants should avoid doing anything they wouldn't feel comfortable doing while sitting together in a conference room. It erodes the sense of everyone's virtual presence when meeting participants have side conversations, engage in obvious and distracting tasks, or disable their cameras.

Turning off a camera (thereby creating the Black Screen of Non-Attention) is akin to walking out of the room during an on-site meeting. Sometimes a meeting participant will need to leave, and then turning off the camera makes sense—but the team member should excuse himself or herself courteously, as they would in an on-site meeting, not just "blink out."

Leaders should work with their teams to establish these types of expectations and guidelines as part of their virtual meeting planning and protocols (see Chapter 3 for more on this).

Communicating from a distance, with the proper tools and right skills, won't be as burdensome as many have experienced it in the past. Distance dialogue will continue to be a pervasive part of the communication, team interaction, and collaboration landscape in the expanding virtual workplace.

Leaders will increasingly be sharing information, resolving problems, nurturing innovation, and strengthening team performance from a distance. Communicating clearly and efficiently with dispersed team members and helping hybrid teams work well together are integral to the success of those who lead today and into the future.

3

ENGAGING FOR RESULTS IN REMOTE MEETINGS AND PRESENTATIONS

Humorist Dave Barry once said, "If you had to identify, in one word, the reason why the human race has not achieved, and never will achieve, its full potential, that word would be 'meetings.'" Yet, the world of work seems to revolve around meetings. There are meetings for everything from brainstorming the company's strategy to planning the next holiday party. Despite always-evolving devices and apps, we will still have meetings to get things done. With the options for gathering together in the on-site workplace increasingly limited, how can virtual meetings be as productive as, or even more productive than, face-to-face meetings?

In this chapter, we'll examine the ways to use technology to effectively lead virtual meetings. Some technology tools are better than others, depending on the purpose or objectives of the meeting. For example, if a leader is conducting a one-on-one meeting with a direct report to discuss the team member's performance, would it be more effective to talk to the associate on the phone, via video, or meet face-to-face? Most people prefer face-to-face. When that's not possible, a video meeting is the best alternative. It's important to see how the team member responds with their body language as cues for confusion, resistance, agreement, or commitment. The team member may say one thing and nonverbally signal something very different, and that's harder to identify without seeing those cues.

If you're thinking that all meetings are best done in-person, we challenge that notion. Presentations are often more effective when done virtually. If you were in a meeting or a training session with a large number of participants, would you want to be in the back of a large conference room squinting at the images projected to the screen at the front? What if

> "In-person meetings are overrated. Even work I used to travel for can be effectively done online."

everyone was actively using all the functionality of web conferencing to chat, ask questions, provide group feedback in real time, and interact with the information presented? With the right planning and use of the right tools, virtual meetings can be better for many purposes than in-person gatherings.

> **Leaders can leverage remote meetings to get the same or better results than in-person meetings.**

Some of the advice found here will hopefully improve your meetings whether you're conducting them in-person or online. Other guidance may apply just to the virtual environment. Apply these tips in whatever way best helps you to engage others and get better results.

We start by taking a look at the most used technology, the good ol' fashioned conference call.

CONFERENCE CALLS

We admit, we really don't like conference calls. Conference calls may be one of the most cumbersome forms of human communication. Why?

Conference calls are inefficient because they cause frequent *audio collisions* between participants. Audio collisions are common when people try to talk over each other. Anyone who has ever been on a conference call is familiar with the following scenario:

Person 1: OK, I think we should…

Person 2 (speaking at the exact same time): Well, what if we…

Both pause as they realize someone else was talking.

Person 1: I'm sorry, you go ahead.

Person 2 (speaking at the exact same time): Apologies. You go first.

Another awkward pause as both wait for the other person to start.

Person 1: As I was saying…

Person 2 (speaking at the exact same time): OK, so why don't we…

And on it goes.

Obviously, a lot of this would be mitigated if the participants could see each other and watch for the visual cues that indicate a person is about to speak. The first rule of virtual meetings should be to use video whenever possible to read body language, signal with gestures, or see facial expressions to make meetings run more effectively. But what if team members can't use video or participants refuse to use the video option? The inefficiencies due to audio collisions and interruptions can make an audio-only meeting relatively unproductive.

IN OUR EXPERIENCE...

In an experiment conducted in collaboration with Dr. Evan Offstein at Frostburg State University in Maryland, one of the authors studied how people interact when they can't see each other and how simple techniques can make the interaction better.

Fourteen participants (students and faculty) were separated into smaller groups, placed at a table with partitions so they could not see each other, and given topics to discuss. Observers watched the interactions. Groups were then given new topics and simple instructions. In the center of the table between the partitions was a small ball. If anyone wanted to speak, they would have to take the ball. When they were done talking, the ball was placed back at the center, and another participant could take it to speak.

In participant interviews that followed, they unanimously felt that their communication was much more efficient in the second round than in the first. There were no interruptions and no audio collisions. Some of the participants even said they felt more empowered by having the ball present in the second round.

Although the sample size in this experiment wasn't large enough to conclusively prove results, the exercise seemed to support the idea that virtual meetings need more structure than face-to-face meetings.

While many virtual meeting apps have functionality that allows participants to raise their virtual hand, this doesn't mean people will use it or not continue to talk over each other. The meeting organizer or facilitator has to provide instructions at the outset and clarify which functionality will be used to let participants speak. Hopping on a call and letting it run in freeform with no ground rules is a recipe for inefficiency and frustration.

VIDEO MEETINGS AND CONFERENCE CALLS

To help leaders run their next meeting more effectively, whether it is a conference call or video meeting, we offer the following tips:

1. **Prepare.** In the last chapter we emphasized the value of planning communications, but it's important enough to repeat it here. How many times have you jumped into a virtual meeting and felt like the meeting facilitator was winging it? The same rules for leading a face-to-face meeting apply to video meetings and conference calls: meeting leaders should spend the necessary time preparing for the meeting, know what they want to accomplish, what questions need to be answered, what discussions may occur, etc. More preparation may be needed just to ensure everyone stays engaged. Regardless of the type of meeting—information sharing, planning, or brainstorming—leaders need to be prepared.

   > "Because you have to more purposeful in scheduling meetings, some of our communications have actually improved."

2. **Manage the attendee list.** How many people will be in the meeting? Are all of the invited participants needed? Will everyone be able to interact? We have been in meetings with approximately 30 – 50 attendees and often wonder if there is a better way for mass communication or information-sharing sessions. If leaders are announcing a company-wide change that's sure to generate a lot of questions, it might make sense

to invite whole departments. But in general, it's best to limit meetings to a size that allows everyone to participate.

3. **Go beyond the agenda; establish goals and objectives.** For many meetings, it's common to send out the agenda beforehand. We've seen many meeting organizers even include the time allotted for each agenda item. This is a good practice, but we've been in far too many meetings where the agenda was not followed. We are not implying that meeting facilitators should abandon this practice, but goals and objectives are more important. At a minimum, pick the "Top 3" for the meeting. Before everyone adjourns and moves to the next meeting, what are the top three things to be decided? Alternatively, what are the top three actions the team needs to take? Or what are the top three things participants should remember?

4. **Start on time.** This is not about punctuality; this is about productivity. It's amazing how few meetings actually start close to the meeting time. Forget right on time. We're talking within five minutes of the planned start time. What happens when meetings don't start on time? Participants hit the mute button and begin multitasking. The meeting organizer has already lost participants before the meeting has begun. Participants may briefly come off mute to introduce themselves, but they are likely going back to their email shortly thereafter.

5. **Master meeting technology.** Similar to #4 above, too much time is often lost at the beginning of a meeting because the leader and participants are trying to get the technology to work (i.e., signing in, screen sharing, etc.). Additionally, meeting applications have a wealth of functionality to engage team members (see Chapter 7). More often than not, leaders fail to leverage these capabilities to make the meeting more efficient and engaging. Everyone should take some time to practice and learn all the details of the meeting technology being used by their organization.

> "Not everyone is equally computer savvy and not everyone wants to admit it. A warm, safe environment is essential."

6. **Keep everyone engaged.** Encourage participation from all attendees. Call on random participants to force engagement or start off with some easy, "softball" questions to get participants to speak up. Be willing to call their attention back to the task at hand. If you can see that multiple participants' minds are wandering off, it might be time for a break.

7. **Level the playing field.** It is always tricky when some team members are physically located together, and others are remote. All too often, the people in the conference room discuss something and, in the last few minutes of the meeting, someone will ask, "Does anyone on the phone have something to add?" It's no wonder that some remote team members feel alienated! Pay extra attention to

> If you have difficulty facilitating a hybrid team, make everyone remote.

remote participants. As the meeting facilitator, ask them to be the first to weigh in on a subject. You might need to build a few stops or pause points in the agenda to specifically request input from the remote participants.

Alternatively, if the majority of the participants are remote, consider making all participants call into the meeting so everyone is remote. Although the facilitator may have to manage the meeting to prevent more audio collisions, the benefit is that all participants will be equal. At a minimum, prioritize remote participants first, allowing them to voice questions or ideas before the in-person attendees.

8. **Stay on track and use a "parking lot."** Like all meetings, conference calls can digress quickly, especially if there are a few vocal people trying to steer the meeting. Don't be afraid to course correct. If the conversation gets off topic, document the issue, assign someone the action to follow up. Put the issue in the 'parking lot' of ideas and return to the meeting topic.

9. **Recap the Actions.** The key word is "actions." Summarizing the meeting at the end of the call is always a best practice, but more importantly, facilitators need to make sure all the actions are documented, assigned owners, and a deadline established for completion of each action before the meeting concludes. Meetings that end without actions are a nice get-together at best but not terribly useful.

10. **Follow Up.** Based on the documented actions, the meeting leader should follow up and update the team on progress. No, this doesn't necessarily mean another conference call. There are a number of ways to do this outside of holding a meeting (i.e., email, scorecards, wikis, etc.). Remember that the follow through is what adds value.

PRESENTING, TRAINING, AND SHARING INFORMATION

Leaders are often presenting information and, in some cases, training their teams. Regardless of whether they are presenting to the senior executive team, formally training new hires, or just sharing information with their team, the virtual experience is different than when they're face-to-face. Here is some guidance for leaders before the "Share Screen" option is clicked on the meeting app.

❖ **Ensure everyone is speaking the same (company) language**

Different groups or functions within an organization often use a different set of terms or language. The terminology from the legal department is typically different than what is used in the IT department. If this is a potential issue, it may be helpful for the leader to spend a few minutes at the outset providing an overview of any unfamiliar terms that might be used. Perhaps a quick reference list provided to all team members would help, as well.

To illustrate this point on how important the language we use can be, there's an old story about a US business that was acquired by a British company. The US leaders, anxious to keep their business, presented several initiatives and projects to their new boss. The head British leader responded to each project review with the word, "Brilliant." The US leaders, not realizing that this was the equivalent of saying "interesting," misinterpreted it as the go-ahead to begin work. A few months and a few million dollars later, the US leaders were shocked when all work was stopped, and they were reprimanded for wasting company funds. The point is, when we communicate in the virtual workplace, or just across functional departments or geographic lines for that matter, there are many things we take for granted.

❖ Know your audience

"Sixty minutes into a 90-minute presentation, I realize that the audience is much more experienced and wants much more detailed information than I'm providing," one person shared with us. *"The simplified presentation I designed was for novices."*

If video is not used and the presenter can't see the expression on the faces of people in the audience, he or she may not know if they are hitting the mark until it is too late. Even if video is used, the meeting app may shrink the participants' video screen down to a miniscule size while the presenter is screen-sharing, so it's hard to read the expressions

> "I enjoyed online teaching more than expected. It helped to have had a pre-existing relationship with the students before we went virtual."

71

of the participants. Presenters need to do their homework and know their audience – their experience level, the number of participants, and their needs. If possible, the presenter should talk to some of the participants beforehand.

❖ Maximize the images and minimize the text

Most people are visual. Pictures or images will get the message across better than text. Text should be kept to a bare minimum. The rest can be kept in the speaker notes. If a presenter were standing in front of a group of people, the presenter could talk through lots of text, but online this is likely to bore people and cause them to lose focus. Presenters should practice using the annotation functionality in their meeting app. It will help focus the attention of the participants and keep them engaged.

❖ Keep the pace, but don't race

People speaking online tend to rush through their content. Dead airtime can seem much longer than it is, and you might feel the need to fill the void with more words. Relax. Take a breath. Rehearse your presentation so you know how much time it takes to get through it and keep your eye on the clock - literally. One benefit of presenting online is that the presenter can have notes, like cue cards, or a large timer behind the webcam where no one else but the presenter will see it. The small clock on the laptop or monitor screen often goes unnoticed, so having a larger clock can help keep the presenter on track.

❖ Use gestures (even when people can't see them)

Why use gestures when participants can't see body language? Using a little body movement and hand gestures will naturally change the inflection in the presenter's voice, avoiding a monotone delivery. Gestures help raise the energy level of the speaker, contributing to the interest level of meeting participants.

❖ Boost the Q&A

Most presentations allow for some questions at the end. Nothing is worse than allotting some time for discussion and all the presenter hears is virtual crickets. Some participants feel awkward asking questions when they don't know or can't see the other attendees. Presenters can help get this going by preparing 4-5 questions of their own that they think participants would likely ask to help get the discussion going. If they've done their homework from the Know Your Audience tip above, this should be easy to do.

❖ Remember the "seven-minute rule"

In the words of an experienced corporate trainer with thousands of hours of experience teaching online, "You only have seven minutes until they're asleep." The trainer's advice: constantly engage your audience. If you go more than about seven minutes without engaging them, then you've lost them. Presenters need to intentionally build engagement points into their

> Engage your audience early and often... or you will lose them!

presentation as reminders to themselves to engage the audience. This could be as blatant as posing a question on the slide to the audience or as subtle as creating a small icon in the corner of the slide just as a visual reminder.

In some cases, use of a remote meeting app can be more effective than an in-person gathering. Meeting apps have functionality, like polling, that can be used to require participants to engage. Alternatively, participants can interact by use of the chat function, sharing their screens, using the "raise hand" functionality, or using the annotation tools in the meeting app.

But what if the remote meeting app doesn't have these capabilities? Presenters can deploy creative techniques, such as asking participants to hold up a hand or sign. In the simplest scenario, meeting leaders can call on participants for questions, suggestions, and sharing of information.

MEETINGS WITH A LARGE NUMBER OF PARTICIPANTS

People tend to agree that a virtual meeting with a small number of participants is easier to facilitate than a meeting with a large number of participants. Scheduling meetings with a high number of in-person attendees is becoming less practical due to space and travel constraints and less attractive when virtual options are available. It may be more challenging, but a large virtual group can be managed effectively with practice and effective use tools within the appropriate virtual meeting platform.

"I facilitate a bi-weekly call for our company's new program introduction process," one manager for a Fortune 500 tech company told us. "As new service programs go through various stages of development, decision makers would meet at specific milestones to approve the program and allow it to progress to the next stage or send it back for more work. Eighteen separate stakeholder groups would listen to the program team make their pitch and then a representative from each group would ask any questions or make comments before approving or rejecting the program. It was not uncommon for up to 50 people to attend the virtual meeting in addition to the decision makers."

The meeting participants, we learned, were scattered across the globe so it was not possible to meet in the same room at the same time even if their travel budgets were limitless. How did they do it?

"It all boils down to meeting management and technology," the manager said. He reiterated our tip about knowing your audience. "Not every participant may be equal, and I'm not necessarily referring to their title or rank within the organization. Some may be subject matter experts and provide key input to direct questions. Others may be decision-makers. And others may be just lurking, listening in for general information. Know who's coming, and more importantly, what you want or expect from them."

Corporate learning and development teams, trainers, department leads, and remote leaders report might benefit from keeping the following nuances in mind when leading large remote meetings:

❖ Spare the lecture, get to the discussion

Many people we interviewed agreed that if a large audience isn't engaged quickly, achieving attendee engagement is quite difficult. This reminded us of the "seven-minute rule" we mentioned earlier. The same applies to large groups. Meeting facilitators may not be able to use all of the interactive functionality found in their remote meeting platform. For example, having over 100 participants trying to annotate something on the screen at once would be a mess. However, the polling function or using emoticons or the "raise hand" function is a quick way to pulse-check the audience. Presenters can also utilize breakout groups to create smaller groups that facilitate more engaging discussion.

Some remote meeting applications have an *attention indicator* that will show the facilitator, via a "ZZZ" icon, when a participant is no longer viewing their screen and has gone into another application. It's a helpful feature for presenters to know who to re-engage. Or if too many people have turned away, the presenter can pull everyone back in by shifting gears with a question, poll, or new topic.)

❖ It may take two

It's often hard for the presenter to focus both on the information being presented and to manage the meeting app or the interactions within the meeting. If possible, having another participant or moderator manage the chat and Q&A functions in the meeting app while the leader presents can make things run a lot smoother. Having co-facilitators will ensure questions are answered without breaking the flow of the presentation, information is disseminated, or if someone is having technical issues, they can get help without interrupting the meeting.

❖ Manage the chaos

Large virtual meetings can get a little unruly. Good meeting technology helps by giving the meeting leader the ability to mute some or all participants, allow others to signal that they want to speak, or let people ask questions through a chat feature. Regardless of the virtual meeting platform being used, meeting facilitators can help by establishing ground rules and enforcing time management.

Although technology continues to change at an ever-increasing pace, it has still not changed the fact that we have a human need to interact and share ideas in real time to get work done. The meeting applications and software available today are fantastic tools in the hands of the meeting leader. However, the tool is only as good as the person using it. A hammer can damage as much as it builds in the hands of the novice or careless wielder. The meeting leader is the one who ensures that the meeting is engaging and effective. Even with the most basic remote meeting technology, such as the conference call, a good leader can

> Master your meeting apps and technology, but also don't forget to be a strong facilitator.

guarantee a positive outcome if that leader makes the conscious effort to prepare for the meeting, engage all the participants, and follow through with actions as agreed.

IN OUR EXPERIENCE

One leader explained to us how he handles large meetings with more than 100 participants.

"The participants are broken down into 3 tiers. The first tier is the senior level executives or key decision makers. These participants will be expecting to present, make statements, or make decisions during the meeting. The second tier is the subject matter experts. They may be expected to speak or present based on the topic at hand. The last tier are all other participants that are attending to listen in and stay informed. They may submit questions prior to the meeting or can use the chat function in the meeting app if there is a moderator monitoring the chat. The meeting facilitator notifies the participants which tier they are in when the meeting agenda and other related meeting information is published. This structure helps keep the meeting on track and from spinning out of control due to enormous number of attendees."

4

HIRING AND ONBOARDING REMOTELY

"I would never hire anyone I couldn't meet face-to-face," one senior manager told us while sitting in his company headquarters surrounded by thousands of employees moving about. "I have to be able to shake their hand and look them in the eye."

This conversation was just a few years after Marissa Mayer, then CEO of Yahoo, sent out her infamous email to employees that effectively ended the company's telework program. Even companies that produced the technology that made remote work possible, such as IBM, were following suit and reining in remote workers by calling them back to the office.

The majority of leaders we interviewed believed that it was a necessity to bring new team members into the organization in-person. In fact, by 2018 only one quarter of companies were onboarding new hires online to some degree. Furthermore, while some companies used phone interviews or video conferencing to screen candidates, almost all of the companies we spoke with relied on at least meeting a job candidate in-person prior to making an offer.

What a difference a few years can make.

GETTING THE RIGHT TALENT

In the landmark book, *Good to Great*, Jim Collins argued that one of the first things great companies do is get "the right people on the bus" before deciding where to drive it. Finding the right talent is paramount to the success of the enterprise, even before the company sets its strategic direction or vision.

Finding the right people is one of the most important tasks for a leader.

The long processes involved in bringing in new talent and embedding it into the organization typically include recruiting, hiring/selection, onboarding, and training. Only recruiting has adopted online as a norm, because of online job boards, hiring algorithms, and HR bots. The other components of the talent acquisition process tended to be more old school (in-person, face-to-face) methods – until recently. Let's begin with the hiring process.

Recruiting and hiring employees with competencies to enable remote working should be important to all leaders, regardless of whether their team members have been accustomed to working on-site. Over the past couple of decades, remote working has steadily gained ground. Therefore, all team members will need to master some basic remote work competencies.

> The workplace is changing—everyone needs remote work competencies.

What makes a good remote worker?

We posed this question to leaders of remote and hybrid teams. We expected to uncover unique characteristics that would make remote workers stand out from associates that head to the office on a daily basis. What we discovered is that many of the characteristics mentioned by our survey respondents were important, regardless of whether a team member was remote or in the physical workspace. However, the traits listed below become even more important as the team becomes more dispersed and increasingly function as a fluid hybrid team.

❖ **Problem solving/resourcefulness**

Remote team members must be able to solve problems on their own. It can be a little more challenging than asking someone in the office or cubicle next door for help. Remote workers have to work with autonomy and, in some cases, fend for themselves. From handling the technical challenges that may arise in their home office to navigating the virtual workplace, remote workers should be able to work through problems and find solutions on their own. Remote employees must be able to use whatever resources they have available to overcome obstacles or take the initiative to reach out for help.

❖ Communication skills (verbal and written)

Remote workers communicate primarily over email, phone, and video, so written and verbal communication skills are an obvious necessity. Remote team members need to be proficient in these remote

"Good communication skills are invaluable!"

workplace tools, and they may also need to comfortable using social platforms, collaboration software, and document sharing. There is no shortage of communication and collaboration tools available to organizations; using them in ways that contribute to productivity will be increasingly important. Hiring managers may require a candidate to have experience or at least familiarity with tools commonly used in the organization, or leaders may expect candidates to have the ability to learn quickly and adapt to new communication methods.

❖ Self-discipline/organization

The number one challenge we heard from people while they were working from home during the COVID-19 pandemic was dealing with distractions (we talk more about this in Chapter 8). The pandemic provided additional distractions, such as kids learning from home or spouses and partners also working from home. However, even without these extra hurdles, many people are easily distracted by domestic chores, the allure of streaming video, the call of the sofa, the persistent temptation to visit the refrigerator, or the tendency to surf the Internet for non-work reasons. Alternatively, some lack the ability to create and follow a daily plan. Good remote employees effectively manage their time, focus on the tasks that need their attention, and meet deadlines.

❖ Motivation

Closely aligned with self-discipline is motivation. Many team members reported to us that one of the biggest challenges working from home was staying motivated. Feelings of isolation and the lack of actual face-to-face interactions with colleagues can weigh on some team members more than others. Some people

> **Staying motivated while working remotely is one of the most oft cited challenges of remote work.**

need the energy of others around them, while others are more than comfortable receiving guidance and just "getting it done" without the distraction of personal interactions.

Remote team members should be self-directed in order to accomplish tasks. Performance reviews, professional references, and assessment exercises can provide a leader with insight on the degree to which a job candidate for a remote position is likely to take initiative and be self-directed. Ask references and seek data from interviews about the candidate's past work environment, team dynamics, and individual work style to assess the candidate's skill and style fit with the new work environment.

❖ Assertiveness

Extroverts, who may shy away from remote work because it will make them feel isolated, might actually make great remote workers. Why? Extroverts possess the other quality remote workers need: Assertiveness.

Historically, there was a misconception that remote work was best for *heads down* activities, i.e., work tasks that could be done in a silo and didn't require the team member to engage with anyone else. That made introverts seem more suited for the solitary life of a remote worker. But when you are dealing with people through cyberspace, it's easy for others to forget you're there unless you make your presence known (a.k.a. "out of sight, out of mind").

Remote workers need to build a virtual presence and ensure others remember they are part of the team. This requires the assertiveness of a more extroverted personality.

❖ Relationship oriented

Perhaps even more important than specific knowledge areas, employees should be able to build virtual relationships and be able to complete assignments leveraging a team or network of collaborators. In today's hyper-connected workplace, no team member is a soloist. Almost everyone has to work within or lead a team at some point. And increasingly people are working in cross-functional or matrixed project teams in addition to their primary team.

Team building when team members are just voices on a teleconference line or small images on a computer screen can be daunting, and it takes skill and talent to overcome distance to pull the team together. Remote workers typically rely on a mix of relationships with team members and other collaborators to get their jobs done.

❖ Emotional intelligence

Ideally, all team members are self-aware, socially aware, and have the ability to correctly recognize their emotions and the emotions of those around them. This ability is known as emotional intelligence.

Leaders managing over distance don't have the day-to-day benefit of personally witnessing subtle behavior changes or reading non-verbal cues like body language. Remote workers need to stay connected and be able to read 'between the lines' (see more on this in Chapters 1 and 2).

> **Learning how to build relationships virtually can be more important than technical skills.**

❖ Experience

It always helps to have experience. Not just subject matter expertise but also the experience of working remotely. The COVID-19 pandemic gave most leaders and team members a chance to work remotely for at least a short period (and much longer for some). This experience can help leaders tasked with onboarding new team members explore how the candidate has previously handled isolation, distractions, interactions with other team members, and the ability to get work done.

INTERVIEWING AND HIRING

Despite the global experience of remote-work-by-necessity during the COVID-19 pandemic, many leaders are still uncomfortable hiring a new associate they have never met face-to-face and may be even more reluctant to hire someone they've never seen at least on video.

If you are hesitant to hire someone you can't, and may never, physically meet, consider why you are so apprehensive. Is it because you've always interviewed in-person and the process is familiar? Do you believe you are a good judge of character and can tell by looking at someone whether they are fit for the role? Do you think you observe someone's body language and determine whether they will align with the organization's culture? It might be worth considering how much is actually missed or misinterpreted by traditional ways of interviewing candidates.

Peter Capelli, a professor of management at the University of Pennsylvania, was quoted by *The Wall Street Journal*, saying that most companies are "so bad at interviewing, and the interviews are so full of bias, that it's not crazy to just ignore them altogether. (Lucas) For many business leaders, eliminating the interview process altogether may seem extreme, but Capelli brings up an excellent point.

Interviews are full of bias, yet hiring managers usually ignore their own preconceived beliefs or overestimate their ability to be objective. People may equate interview bias with stereotyping or racial and gender bias, but think about the halo effect, which occurs when interviewers allow a strong trait to overshadow the candidate's weaker traits; the recency effect, resulting when hiring managers may recall the most recent job candidates better than previous ones, or even the contrast effect, which occurs when strong candidates that interview after weaker candidates are seen in an overly positive light.

Let's face it—most hiring managers are probably not as good at interviewing as they think they are. This may explain why organizations are increasingly leveraging online skills assessments, behavioral simulations, and personality tests to select the right candidates. When a candidate usually makes it to the in-person interviewing stage, interviewers are more likely assessing the candidate's cultural fit and ability to work within the team. (Note, this is also where affinity bias plays a strong role. We tend to prefer those that are like ourselves.)

> Virtual hiring can help reduce some of the natural bias that occurs in the process.

Can hiring virtually help leaders make better choices than hiring in-person? Leaders should think about how they will interact with the candidate if the candidate becomes part of the team. Will the candidate be physically located with the team or will interactions be primarily virtual or hybrid? If the team members hired will interact with others primarily in a virtual environment (video or phone interactions), meeting in-person can actually be a little misleading. The normal paradigm is reversed: if someone interviews really well in-person, it doesn't necessarily mean they will have a good virtual presence.

IN OUR EXPERIENCE...

"It was like the person we hired was totally different than the one we met," one hiring manager complained to us. The candidate had been hired as an analyst a few months prior and was working remotely full-time in another state distant from the manager. "We flew the candidate in for in-person interviews after the initial phone screen. During the interview process, I thought he was very intelligent and thoughtful, maybe a little on the introverted side. That was okay in my mind since the job was mostly analyzing data. However, we interacted mostly over email and conference calls. On group conference calls, he never said a word, and we quickly forgot he was there sometimes. Over email he was responsive, but his style of writing was very abrupt. I really don't believe he was trying to be rude. He was just very direct, and that put a lot of people off."

We are not implying that the organization should avoid meeting a candidate in-person. However, hiring managers may get a better idea of how the candidate will perform if the interview style and setting mimic the work environment in which the team member will function.

Here are a few suggestions for hiring managers of candidates who will likely work as a remote or hybrid team member:

❖ **Create a consistent remote interviewing experience.** We've witnessed organizations put a lot of effort and thought into their on-site interview process, but when it comes to conducting remote interviews, it feels like they are running a casual, ad hoc meeting. The candidate experience should not vary that much regardless of whether the candidate is virtual or in-person.

❖ **Prepare for the interview.** The biggest problem in the interview process is lack of preparation. (Trull) Recognizing that candidate success on the job is not only about job qualifications, but also about how a candidate will work with others, hiring managers should think about how the candidate will work in a remote or fluid hybrid environment. Hiring managers should read through the candidate's resume, references, and any other material they may have on the candidate. Are the key competencies and experiences the hiring manager is looking for easily identifiable in the candidate's reference material? If not, the hiring manager should be prepared to specifically probe into those areas (see Appendix B for Interview Questions for Remote Work).

❖ **Use video.** Video has become ubiquitous in today's work world. Our advice is to make sure the video quality is good. High-end, life-size telepresence systems can make leaders feel like they are in the room with the candidate, but most people still rely on webcams. Decide which platform will be used and use it consistently to develop proficiency. Conduct a test run prior to the interview to make sure there are no technical issues. Additionally, hiring managers should send out instructions to the candidate on how to log in into the video app, any passwords that will be used, and basic troubleshooting tips.

> "We did a video interview, and the app didn't work well with the candidate's computer. Everything was in shades of green. It's hard to look at someone who looks like the Hulk."

❖ **Listen to how they say things, not just what they say.** How is the candidate's verbal communication? Is the candidate clear and concise? Can s/he explain abstract ideas? This is especially important if the new hire is expected to regularly interact with others over teleconference or via video meetings.

❖ **Monitor written communication.** We rely so much on the verbal and visual exchange of information when we interview that we often don't verify a candidate's written communication. Hiring managers shouldn't be afraid to email candidates after the interview with a follow up question or two to elicit an email from them. Is it too informal? Is it too wordy and not to the point? This may be the first glimpse at a candidate's written communication skills. If written skills are a critical part of the job, this is a good example of when a more formal exercise or simulation would be appropriate.

❖ **Create a professional appearance.** Candidates will judge the company based on the interview experience and behaviors of the interviewers. Interviewers should present a professional appearance and be cognizant of the appearance of their home office if that is the backdrop for the video interview.

❖ **If there are technical glitches, how does the candidate handle them?** We've all had technical difficulties working remotely. For us, this has occurred from time to time when a candidate had trouble calling in. One of us once had a candidate experience trouble calling in (for whatever reason), and the call dropped after 5 minutes. He sent an email to the recruiter asking to reschedule, in spite of having back-up cell phone and office phone numbers, as well as the recruiter's phone number. Working remotely often requires being somewhat resourceful and self-reliant to work through the numerous challenges that are bound to arise. If a candidate can't work through issues for an interview, how well do you think they'll do it on the job?

❖ **Provide an opportunity for virtual social gatherings.** It's common with some on-site interviews for candidates to have an opportunity to meet team members not directly involved in the interview process. This is sometimes done over coffee or lunch. It's a chance to see how the candidate interacts with others and fits into the culture. In a remote setting, this is obviously more challenging, but not impossible.

Hiring managers can create opportunities for remote candidates to meet the team in an informal video session or sit in on a virtual team meeting.

❖ **Don't be afraid to ask for feedback.** Hiring managers should ask remote candidates for feedback on the interview process. This can be done via a survey or follow up email. Candidate feedback can be used to further refine and improve the process.

ONBOARDING

One of the most common challenges we heard from senior leaders we surveyed related to onboarding new associates without any face-to-face interaction. Although most organizations have some capabilities to enable employees to work remotely, most struggle with remote onboarding.

Considering that three-quarters of CFOs plan to shift at least some of their on-site employees to permanent remote work arrangements after the COVID-19 pandemic is over, organizations will need to implement effective, ongoing virtual onboarding practices. (Gartner)

Before we go any further, we need to define employee onboarding. Many organizations equate onboarding to new hire orientation or the completion of required documents when a new associate joins the organization. Others define the onboarding

> Onboarding processes may vary but are critical to the success of new hires.

process from pre-hire activities, such as systems access and issuing of equipment, through new hire training and a probationary performance period.

Because of the variations on how organizations define the starting and ending points of the onboarding process, it can be as little as one day or as long as 90-120 days. For our purposes, let's consider that onboarding begins when a new hire accepts the position and ends when a new employee has all the necessary tools, skills, and training to be a productive team member.
Onboarding may include:

- Day 1 Readiness (systems access, equipment/asset issue)

- Mandatory compliance training (i.e., safety, security, data protection, diversity, workplace harassment, etc.)

- Business processes and employee information (i.e., compensation & benefits, HR info)

- Site specific procedures or policies (site orientation)

- Company vision, mission, values, culture

- Soft skills training

- Technical/tools training

- Job shadowing

A quality onboarding experience is important for all employees in regard to their productivity and retention. Glassdoor.com claims that a positive onboarding experience can improve new employee productivity by 70%. (Laurano) Another study showed that employees who underwent a structured onboarding program were almost 60% more likely to be with the organization after 3 years. (Hirsch)

However, 88% of employees surveyed by Gallup reported their employers don't provide a good onboarding program. (Gallup) This may have something to do with the fact that a majority of companies associate onboarding with completing mandatory HR paperwork. (Filipkowski)

Yikes! These statistics show that onboarding is immensely important to the organization, yet most organizations fail to leverage its potential as an efficient way to improve new hire effectiveness and retention. The onboarding experience may be even more important to remote and hybrid workers who can quickly feel lost or marginalized if leaders don't engage with them early.

READY, DAY 1

When a candidate accepts an offer and receives a start date, a lot goes on behind the scenes to make sure the new hire is ready for onboarding and not dragged down or distracted by administrative or logistical matters. Various departments—Information Technology, Security, Human Resources, Finance, Asset Management—work together to ensure readiness. Items on the readiness checklist may include:

- Network credentials, i.e. username and password
- Company email address

- Access to certain systems, tools, or internal sites (Typically, new hires are matched to certain job profiles which have role-based security, allowing access to the appropriate areas within the company.)

- Equipment procurement, i.e. PC and other office equipment

- Phone (phone extension, soft phone, cell phone, or app deployed to personal cell phone)

- Required documentation, such as non-disclosure agreements, acknowledgements, etc.

- Instructions for Day 1 sent to new hire

We spoke with one executive overseeing the call center for a Fortune 500 company about his experience during COVID-19.

> *"I'm not going to lie. We struggled at the beginning," he said. "Although we had a small percentage of call center agents already working from home, we weren't prepared to immediately deploy 100 percent of our workforce."*

He further explained that when a candidate accepted an offer and the background check was complete, there were established processes already in place to request network access, a personal email address, and access to various areas behind the firewall.

> *"The first showstopper was around company-issued equipment," he said. "Even with the small group that was working from home prior to the pandemic, we required that they come into the office on day one and*

then complete 4 weeks of training in-person, followed by working on the floor for a couple of months before they went to their home office. Equipment, such as laptops and headsets, was not issued until the beginning of the second week of training. Once the office building was shut down, not only did we have to figure out how to ship equipment to new hires, but training had to shift from 100 people in a classroom to 100 percent virtual."

The company decided to outsource their asset management, relying on a third party to ship and track equipment. That provider handled scenarios such as when an associate didn't successfully complete the new hire training. In this case, the vendor collected all the equipment that had been issued. However, the company had to decide which equipment was issued to new hires and which items would *not* be provided. For example, when call center agents worked in the office, they had dual monitors, keyboard, mouse, phone, access to office supplies, an ergonomically correct chair, etc.

The company agreed to provide computer equipment and monitors but no other resources, such as an office chair or office supplies. (Note: In our research, we found that organizations vary greatly in this regard. Some companies offer a full office setup, while others simply issue a laptop. Some provide a stipend to allow employees to purchase items for their home office, but many others do not.)

> Ensure processes are in place to enable new hire productivity and engagement on Day 1.

"We then worked through the other components of readiness," he said. "When associates were in the office, they had landline phones on their desks. We switched to a softphone on each PC. We made sure everyone had multiple options for video meetings so we could communicate internally with one another. Anything that required an employee signature, from HR paperwork to disclosures, was moved online for digital signature capability. Some of the training was converted to pre-recorded, self-paced training, while other training components were delivered via our video platform. It's still not perfect, but we're getting better at it."

ALL ABOARD

In Chapter 6 we discuss organizational culture in greater detail, but maintaining culture starts with new hire onboarding. Remember that onboarding is more than just orientation. It's an opportunity to introduce new hires to the company's values and expected behaviors (*how* they are expected to get work done, not just *what* is expected to get done).

An onboarding program may include formal training on job related activities, but don't overlook the importance of providing training or discussions that communicate the organizational culture. Sadly, only 39% of employees reported that they received any sort of training on the organization's culture when they were hired, according to one survey. (Zoe)

Aside from training, the biggest influence on how well new hires fit into or adopt the culture, and ultimately how team members perform, is their leader. Leaders must actively participate in the onboarding process. In the call center we mentioned in the previous section, we found that the newly hired team members underwent 4 weeks of classroom training and another several weeks of on-the-job training before even meeting their direct supervisor. In our observations, this is far too late in the process for an initial meeting between leader and team member.

Leaders are vital to onboarding success. Meet new hires as soon as possible.

One of the biggest concerns of a typical new hire is meeting the expectations of the supervisor. Therefore, it's critical that leaders engage with their new team members as early possible.

Technology has made the leader's job easier. Leaders can conduct a video meeting with their new team members on Day 1 to welcome them (no more hunting for conference rooms!). Although a welcome email doesn't hurt to document the initial greeting and expectations, it's best to meet new team members face-to-face over video if a physical meeting is not feasible. One-on-one sessions are a better alternative to group meetings, since a large number of participants on most videoconferencing platforms can shrink the participants into tiny windows on the screen. As a result, leaders can miss nonverbal cues and body language.

For hybrid teams, it's acceptable and natural to meet with some team members in-person if they are on-site and others on video if they are remote. Again, we recommend that these sessions be done one-on-one. If the initial meeting is done as a group, the risk is that the remote team members might feel alienated from the beginning if the leader appears to focus more on the in-person attendees.

Best practices for onboarding include early and ongoing leader engagement. Leaders should regularly engage with team members—as a quick pulse-check to gather feedback, provide additional detailed guidance, or introduce the new associate to the rest of the team. A good rule of thumb is to schedule 30-, 60-, and 90-day check-ins with new employees. Be sure to introduce the new associate to the rest of the team. If the new hire initially meets the team through a group videoconference, arrange for additional, one-on-one video meetings with each team member and other key collaborators throughout the organization.

FINAL THOUGHTS

This chapter covered the key components that make up the talent acquisition and integration process. The first step is to always select the right talent. For remote and hybrid teams, this means the competencies that enable a team member to be successful may be slightly different than those that are necessary in traditional workplace settings. Next, hiring managers should take time to prepare for the interview process and determine the right questions to ask to ensure candidates are equipped to apply targeted competencies in a virtual work environment   (see Appendix B for suggested interview questions).

When candidates have been selected and it's time to bring them into the organization, don't overlook the many logistical requirements to make their first day run smoothly. Think about what you want employees' experience to be on their first day. Then extend that thought to how you want team members to feel after their onboarding process. Should they feel less anxious? Excited to be part of the organization? Ready to be productive? The answers to these questions should never be dependent on whether the team member is remote, works on-site, or both.

5

COACHING AND DEVELOPING REMOTE TEAM MEMBERS

EFFECTIVE REMOTE LEADERSHIP

Leaders serve their teams in a variety of roles, including boss, manager, guide, teacher, supporter, advocate, facilitator, performance director, champion, mentor, and coach. All of these roles require that a leader be a good communicator. Leaders must also be adept at giving and receiving feedback, problem-solving, and building relationships, among other skills. To be successful in the expanding virtual workplace with work-from-anywhere team members and various iterations of hybrid teams, remote leaders must lead with skills that provide or demonstrate:

❖ **Results-based Performance**

A critical aspect of the remote leader's role is to establish clear performance criteria and measurement methods.

101

Every working relationship with team members will be influenced by this. Focusing on results instead of 'face time' or other less tangible factors helps both leaders and their teams be more successful. When team members are dispersed and gather in fluid hybrid configurations, this becomes even more essential. Unambiguous results are an important anchor in bridging the distance between leaders and the team.

Performance-based management is, by far, the most reasonable, consistent, and fair approach to team management—and it .just makes good sense in the virtual workplace.

❖ **Effective Coaching and Feedback**

Team members will, at times, need the guidance, expertise, suggestions, support, and feedback from their leader. This helps them develop their skills, navigate organizational obstacles and politics, and achieve their goals. This is true of any team leader relationship with team members. However, when leading a remote team, leaders should be more mindful of when their coaching and feedback are needed.

> "To build and maintain engagement and motivation, the immediate supervisors touch base with team members more frequently."

As a routine part of the communication patterns between the leader and team members, it's helpful to both create and seek opportunities to coach, offer feedback, and provide support. Feedback and coaching should be timely, targeted, and balanced. It's important for remote team members to understand that their leader is aware of their efforts, understands their challenges, supports their development needs, and values their contributions.

❖ **Clarity of Expectations**

What do remote team members say they value most? Clear, straightforward communication of expectations. Working remotely can leave some team members feeling isolated and detached. Their motivation and focus might diminish over time. Remote leaders can help them overcome these feelings by being very specific about expectations.

If they're going to be productive and satisfied, remote team members will need performance targets to guide their team interactions, project participation, completion of tasks, and behavior standards.

Leaders need their own targets, too, to help them keep up with the desired levels of communication, team interactions, performance coaching, and team development.

❖ **Consistency in Honoring Commitments**

Working with people who honor their commitments contributes to a productive and satisfying work environment. Remote leaders must recognize that this kind of integrity begins with them.

Leading from a distance requires being particularly aware that remote team members might feel unsupported if the leader misses a scheduled call, fails to respond to an email, or doesn't deliver a promised action. A strong history of reliability goes a long way toward minimizing the sense of distance and separation inherent in remote work. If the expectation is that team members are reliable, dependable, and accessible, then the remote leader must model this behavior.

❖ Relationships Built on Trust

As discussed in Chapter 1, trust is a critical component of successful virtual work. Remote leaders need to trust team members to have the ability and motivation to meet their goals. Similarly, remote team members need to trust their leader to provide timely and reliable communication, support, and access to the leader's time and attention. Both the leader and team members must trust their relationships with each other and behave in ways that nurture and support that trust. However, in this area especially, leaders must lead by modeling how trust is established, nurtured, and maintained.

❖ Proficiency with Remote Work Technology

Technology will keep evolving to enable the virtual workplace, but someone on the team needs to keep up with new technological developments and learn to use the latest features, and then demonstrate their functionality by actually using them. That person should be the leader, who should learn everything the communication platforms can do and use them.

When the leader understands remote work technology the best, he or she becomes a valuable resource and advocate in addressing any technological problems that impact the team's effectiveness. This also helps the leader ensure that the right technology tools and digital platforms are provided to the team.

❖ Effective Interpersonal Skills

Much of the success of remote teams is based on the strength of relationships between team members and leaders. Therefore, a significant responsibility falls to the leader to identify, model, and reinforce the interpersonal skills integral to effective relationships within the team. Like most of the skills we've covered, interpersonal skills are always important, but even more important when the leader is remote.

Remote leaders need the ability to communicate, foster team development, confront problems, handle difficult situations, coach for improvement and success, and celebrate achievement using effective interpersonal skills—from a distance——and effectively using all the technology tools available.

❖ Understanding of Remote Work Challenges

The best way to understand and empathize with remote team members' experience is for the leader to sometimes work remotely. If some of team members are distant, and the leader always works from the office, there may not be a good understanding of the frustration remote team members feel, or the simple things that would make their lives easier.

When all team members, including the leader, work remotely some or all of the time, team members are likely to feel better understood and supported, which will make them more successful. When the remote leader and team members are "in the same boat" with technology, it will be easier for the leader to coach them and offer support. Sincerely understanding remote team challenges will also help the leader eliminate barriers to team member success.

MANAGING PERFORMANCE FROM A DISTANCE

As the virtual workplace has evolved and with technology advances that have enabled more work-from-anywhere options, it hasn't been a rosy picture for everyone. While some people struggled to obtain approval to work from home occasionally, others were given mandates to work from home.

Even when organizations allowed remote work, it was not always fully embraced by all managers and supervisors. Team members were sent home but were accompanied by their managers' doubts and concerns. How would they know people were really working?

Employees shared some of these trepidations. How could they prove they were working? What if they were "out of sight, out of mind" and passed over for promotions or new opportunities? How could they get "face time" with a manager whose face was many miles away?

The idea of having to see workers working goes all the way back to the Industrial Age, where production and piece work by workers was measurable and observable. Remnants of that mindset carried into the information age, where we gathered in offices instead of manufacturing plants but continued to believe that the activity we observed was directly related to performance. Of course, the flaw in this thinking is that activity does not constitute results—but business was stuck with the idea that if the boss couldn't see people, they couldn't be managed.

> **Activity does not constitute results.**

And even if leaders could manage distant workers, they certainly couldn't coach them. Think about it—when you've been coached in sports, by teachers, or by managers, it has most likely been a face-to-face encounter. Our bias is to want to "see" the person in a coaching or performance feedback discussion. Yet suddenly, you have become a remote leader, expected to manage and coach from a distance.

The fundamental coaching and development guidelines discussed here are applicable in both face-to-face and remote settings. As leaders increasingly handle these interactions remotely, however, it's helpful to remember that replicating and simulating the in-person

> **Replicate & simulate the in-person experience through remote connections.**

experience through remote connections will provide the best outcome.

If a leader is coaching a team member to improve performance—but the leader can't physically see the team member performing—it's essential to set very specific, measurable goals, and then take the time to monitor progress toward those goals. The leader may be grappling with new, unfamiliar ways to best support team members and address coaching and development needs. But it can be done!

SET PERFORMANCE TARGETS

Leaders need to set specific performance expectations that both they and their team members clearly understand. In this case, the expansion of the virtual workplace has been a good thing for performance management. Why? Because distance demands the type of clarity that has sometimes been lacking in the traditional workplace. Proximity promotes a "we'll know it when we see it" attitude, sometimes justifying the absence of measurable performance targets. This was never a good idea in the on-site workplace, and it just won't work for remote or hybrid teams.

> **"Trying to determine workload accomplishments while distance working has been an issue for us."**

The remote leader needs to establish the associated behavioral expectations for achieving the goals that the leader and the team member set. And it's important to communicate how the team member's performance fits into broader organizational vision, mission, strategy, values, and goals—as well as the team member's personal development goals.

Many organizations rely on the **SMART** formula for goal setting. This approach helps clarify performance targets and how performance will be measured. SMART goals have the following characteristics:

SPECIFIC (clear, short, to the point; not vague)

MEASURABLE (specific criteria for tracking progress; quantitative or qualitative)

ATTAINABLE (achievable with good work)

RELEVANT (within reach, realistic, meaningful, aligned)

TIME-BOUND (clear timeline with target date with sense of urgency)

Establishing performance expectations, deliverables, goals, and deadlines can be a distance communication challenge for remote leaders. Keeping remote teams informed about organizational strategy and translating that to the team and individual team member level usually requires multiple communication methods and a significant time investment by leaders, in addition to the time and effort necessary to establish clear performance targets that are measurable.

Team members need to know where they fit into the big picture, to understand why their contributions are important. Remote team members also need to have a clear understanding of how they can ask for feedback; how they can offer suggestions; and how meeting their performance goals will help them advance.

Most organizations have an established performance management and feedback process with specific timeframes for setting goals and conducting review discussions. Leaders setting performance expectations with remote team members will benefit from planning these discussions. The following basic guidelines will help leaders provide remote team members with the necessary clarity and support in setting performance goals:

1. Review the performance management process.

2. Ask if they have questions or concerns about the process.

3. Discuss organization and department mission/goals.

4. Discuss organization/team/individual needs.

5. Establish performance goals/expectations.

6. Agree on support/development needs.

7. Establish timeframes and dates for interim review and follow-up discussions.

8. Offer support for any needed coaching or assistance.

KEY RELATIONSHIP SKILLS

Building strong relationships with team members is critical to achieving the performance goals that have been set. Handling these discussions from a distance requires a focus on dialogue that provides open opportunities for both sharing and seeking information, feelings, concerns, and commitment. The **LEAD** acronym is a handy reminder of the relationship skills remote leaders need for goal-setting discussions, as well as follow-up coaching and review discussions, as well as follow-up coaching and review discussions.

Listen for commitment, confusion, or concerns.

Encourage the team member's sense of competence.

Ask for their ideas, suggestions, and questions.

Disclose your feelings, viewpoints, and perspectives.

COACHING FOR SUCCESS OR IMPROVEMENT

We are on the cutting edge of a dramatic shift to expanded remote work and on-site/off-site work arrangements. Leaders must help their teams work together to effectively navigate the evolving hybrid team dynamic that was sparked by the pandemic of 2020 and is shaping the future of work.

As remote and fluid hybrid teams face new challenges, there will be plenty of opportunities to anticipate barriers, resistance, and the need for new approaches. These present remote leaders with opportunities to *coach for success* by looking ahead to avoid problems and conflicts.

These discussions "decrease the possibility of performance problems later. Either you or the team member, who may make a specific request for your help, can initiate these discussions. You can incorporate coaching for success discussions when conducting new employee orientations, delegating new assignments, preparing a client response, or creating a new project team." (Dinnocenzo)

Discussions that involve *coaching for improvement* typically involve a performance deviation or shortfall that needs to be corrected. These discussions may occur during regular interim or annual performance reviews, are usually initiated by the leader, and may be a follow-up discussion to a previous coaching intervention. Discussions related to the need for performance improvement are fraught with the potential for more resistance, emotion, and anxiety. And these are the types of dynamics we naturally want to avoid in remote communication. Why?

> **"Performance is an issue when you have to reprimand or improve an employee that you do not see regularly. Disciplinary actions are not easy virtually."**

In spite of easier access to video-based communication that strengthens the leader's ability to see visual cues and to read non-verbal expressions, many leaders are still less comfortable having these more difficult discussions from a distance. However, this is the reality many leaders are now facing, so finding the best ways to approach these discussions helps both the leader and team members minimize discomfort and obstacles to effective communication.

This is achieved both by leveraging technology tools for their best use in establishing a meaningful rapport even while remote (see Chapter 3 for more on this).

Additionally, using effective interaction skills for these types of discussions will help the leader structure the discussion so there's a balance between telling and seeking of information. This ensures that the team member feels heard, the team leader uncovers all the critical information, and an action plan is created.

Leaders always benefit from planning these coaching for success or improvement discussions in advance. If the situation might be particularly challenging, the leader can practice the discussion with a peer, using a role- play format. This allows the leader to refine the approach and planned dialogue, with the extra benefit of insights and feedback from a trusted colleague.

Plan coaching discussions in advance.

Whether the coaching discussion is with an individual team member or with the whole team, leaders can follow these guidelines for the coaching sessions:

1. Clarify the purpose and desired outcomes of the discussion.
Why are we meeting, why is it important, and what needs to be accomplished?

2. Review information you have and ask for additional information and ideas.
Discuss available data, welcome input on additional data, suggestions, obstacles, opportunities.

3. Establish or review performance objectives.
Communicate outcomes, goals, timelines.

4. Discuss ideas and concerns.
Encourage sharing of issues, problems, obstacles, suggestions, solutions.

5. Agree on goals or plan of action.
Confirm WHAT will be done, HOW it will be done and by WHEN; clarify any needs for additional support.

6. Agree on follow-up steps and timeline.
Confirm accountabilities for action and review/follow-up dates.

In some situations—when a team member's performance suddenly changes, or changes within the company are causing problems, or resistance is high—it's especially important for the leader to 'listen between the lines' of what's being said and watch for visual cues that indicate anger or emotional upset. (These signs might be obvious—

> Listen between the lines' and watch for visual cues.

114

tears, abusive language, threats, shouting—but also might be as subtle as crossed arms, sweating, periods of silence, and clenched fists.) Whether the discussion is being held via audio or video connection, the leader must be mindful of signs that emotions are running high, consider if the discussion should be deferred to another time and with a supporting resource. Respond appropriately using these guidelines:

1. Stay calm.

2. Listen objectively and respond with empathy.

3. Ask clarifying questions and seek additional information.

4. Discuss possible courses of action.

5. Summarize and set a time for follow-up.

DEVELOPMENT FROM A DISTANCE

With the right tools and skilled facilitation, online learning can rival the effectiveness of classroom training, and it can offer significant benefits. Online training means decreased travel, lower costs, and improved learner satisfaction. It also can help virtual team members develop skill using a technology platform that they will then use on the job— and this applies to leaders and team members alike. Online leadership training for skills in coaching, managing change, problem solving, listening, and other key leadership competencies will make remote leaders more comfortable using the same technology to apply those skills.

Using the online platform for training and development allows leaders and team members to practice—in a safe environment, where learning is the focus—using the tools that are now important components of team meetings, team member interactions, and team leader communication. Some communication platforms might have features remote leaders have never used; if they get training in using them (or must use them as part of their training), they'll have more valuable tools at their disposal. Fortunately, the tendency to use a fully functional video platform only for audio connections is becoming more rare, as remote leaders and teams gain experience and confidence using video tools.

> **Deliver leadership training in the virtual meeting platform leaders use for team meetings.**

IN OUR EXPERIENCE...

Training delivered via online platform with the 'hidden agenda' to develop capability in using the online platform tools. Training was designed to create multiple opportunities for learners to move into break-out rooms, present small group reports, use the chat feature, share documents, participate in polls, etc.

Some people have been resistant to video meetings in the past. They might feel uncomfortable being on camera or unsure about how to use the video platform functions. Their go-to excuse: It's easier to just use audio rather than activating the video feature. But as employees gain experience in using new technology for meetings, fewer remote teams will use audio-only connections. When the pandemic of 2020 forced vast numbers of people out of the office, most of them quickly figured out how to connect their laptop cameras. They soon discovered how important seeing colleagues is to feeling more connected, less isolated, and more present with each other.

> "We've encouraged use of ALL engagement tools in virtual meeting platforms to increase attention and participation."

Some organizations provide formal training delivered by a skilled facilitator or trainer—but it's the leader's responsibility to handle the day-to-day requirements of ongoing team member development. Remote leaders will find many opportunities to leverage the "just-in-time" and "in-the-moment" learning opportunities dispersed team members need. These might be informal exchanges initiated by a team member ("See that little button that looks like a bicycle horn? What's that for?") or it might require sufficient time and preparation for an effective coaching session, such as when a new piece of equipment arrives, or a new procedure is being introduced.

Leaders should always be listening for a development opportunity or need, such as when a team member:

- Asks for help with a problem or opportunity

- Is uncertain about how to handle a situation

- Expresses frustration with a task or colleague

- Seems overwhelmed or unmotivated

- Demonstrates a lack of motivation

- Is facing a new task, challenge, or project

Likewise, the remote leader is likely to identify team development opportunities when team members are struggling with relationships, project management, collaboration, or team cohesiveness. In any of these cases with team members or the entire team, it's important for the leader to:

- Listen and convey the importance of what's heard by taking notes.

- Ask questions and provide plenty of "air-time" for team members to express feelings and share information.

- Use reflective listening to ensure understanding. ("What I think I'm hearing you say is…")

- Ask team members to suggest actions or solutions.

- Agree on follow-up steps and timeline.

Leaders are increasingly taking responsibility for more formal development for their teams, as well as reinforcement of development and training programs in which team members are engaged. There's good reason for leaders stepping into development initiatives in a more robust way. By doing so, the leader conveys the importance of the development effort and the value the

Leader as trainer = Credible training.

118

leader places on the time invested and the skills or information team members are acquiring. This is especially important as team members are more dispersed and not able as frequently (if at all) to participate in development programs on-site.

It's a wise strategy for leaders to utilize technology tools to create development opportunities for the team to experience together. These are particularly impactful if the leader is leading the learning process. This doesn't need to be an onerous undertaking involving days of time; lengthier learning events are more often best left to human resources or consultants. Where remote leaders can, however, utilize "mini learning" opportunities for the team to share within routine team meetings, the benefits to the team and the remote leader will typically have an excellent return on investment.

TECHNOLOGY FOR REMOTE COACHING AND DEVELOPMENT

Communication tools such as video-based connections, as well as voice calls and other tech resources, are the critical tools remote leaders must use effectively to facilitate ongoing coaching and development. In the "food chain" of remote communication, it has become clear that a video-based connection is the superior way to connect with team members. Many people prefer to learn and process information visually, and video connections are the best way to replicate and simulate the human connections that teams value in the traditional workplace.

There is still room in remote communication for voice-to-voice audio connections—the basic phone call. Calls are quick and don't require as much coordination with the remote team member as a video meeting. The "live" interaction afforded by a phone call is certainly preferable to the non-synchronous alternatives like emails, which don't give you any benefit of experiencing the person's reactions. In Chapter 3, you'll find more information on technology and tips for engaging team members in remote meetings.

6

SUSTAINING CULTURE IN A DISPERSED ORGANIZATION

A mid-sized supply chain company based in the southeast had a reputation as a demanding, fast-paced place to work. When asked to summarize their company's culture in one word, the word employees there used most often was "execute." They knew what their key success metrics were and constantly felt the pressure to meet their targets—even if it meant that relationships would be strained in the process.

This company had the technology to make remote work possible. They even had an established work-from-home policy. However, senior management valued face-to-face interactions. They expected employees to meet in-person to solve problems, instead of just exchanging emails. Employees felt compelled to commute to the office because, if they weren't visible in meetings or seen weaving through the cubicle labyrinth, they wouldn't be making a good impression. Even when the pandemic struck, employees were eager to get back to the office. That changed one morning when an employee called in sick. She had been sick for a few days with a sore throat and runny nose, but still came into the office. Now she had tested positive.

Human Resources jumped into action to avoid a panic among the other employees. How many people had she been in contact with? Would there be an outbreak now within the department … or on the same floor … or in the entire building? Company executives ordered everyone to work from home until other employees could be tested.

It was 2009, and the infected employee had been diagnosed with H1N1, commonly known as "swine flu." Although swine flu was less dangerous than coronavirus, the H1N1 pandemic provides an interesting case study of the way some organizations might react to contagious illness, even when the current pandemic is gone.

After other employees had all tested negative, they slowly returned to the office. Although the business had been forced to immediately pivot to handle their crisis, the company culture never fully changed. A year later, the H1N1 outbreak was just another story in company lore, and all the employees had returned to work on-site again.

However, some employees did notice that things were different. Even though the company's management still favored in-person interactions over virtual ones, they also were more flexible toward employees who needed to occasionally work from home. They had learned that operations could continue seamlessly, even when everyone was not together under one roof.

Organizational culture is that hard-to-define collection of history and habits that helps govern the behavior of all members of the organization. Culture can be the factor that determines how quickly (and successfully) an organization adopts a new initiative or changes in response to external factors. This was a key concern of leaders we surveyed. More than a third of our survey respondents pointed to organizational culture as a key challenge of working remotely. They considered maintaining organizational culture a higher concern than onboarding new hires, collaborating virtually, and even building relationships.

Let's take a look at organizational culture and explore the factors that create and influence it. You'll find ways to maintain and strengthen culture as teams become more fluid.

WHAT IS ORGANIZATIONAL CULTURE, AND WHY SHOULD YOU CARE?

Organizational culture is a somewhat elusive term, with varying definitions. Textbooks commonly describe it as a system of shared beliefs or key characteristics that the organization values. (Robbins)   Others may describe it more as a set of observable behavioral patterns that act as a sort of social control mechanism, reinforcing behaviors consistent with the norms of the organization and discouraging behaviors that deviate. (Watkins)

Each organization might have a dominant culture that spreads across the enterprise, but subcultures also exist within various departments or teams. These subcultures may align with—or in some cases, exist counter to—the overall organizational culture. As a team leader, you might have little influence on the company-wide culture—but you can definitely have a direct impact on your team's subculture.

> Organizational culture can impact the performance of the business.

Think of organizational culture as a powerful undercurrent that influences the organization's operational and financial performance. The culture also determines how those outside the company, including potential hires, perceive the company. Job site Glassdoor reported that more than three-quarters of job seekers would consider an organization's culture before applying for a job. More than half said culture is more important than salary when it comes to job satisfaction. To illustrate the importance of culture, think about the following examples:

- Publix Super Markets, a Florida-based grocery chain, is the largest employee-owned company in the U.S. Its employee-centric culture might help explain why the company boasts margins better than Wal-Mart and other chains. Staff turnover rates are around 5 percent

(Indeed) compared to an industry average turnover rate of almost 49 percent. (Grocerydive)

- Southwest Airlines is well-known for its customer-centric culture that combines hard work with lighthearted fun. Management empowers employees to go out of their way to make customers happy. Prior to the COVID-19 outbreak, Southwest had been profitable for forty-seven consecutive years in an industry where competitors regularly struggled. (Patel)

- In contrast with the two examples above, Uber was considered to have a toxic culture. A key organizational value—"hustlin'"—was founder Travis Kalanick's way to emphasize the relentless pursuit of getting results. Although its unforgiving culture might have helped Uber become the leader in the ride-share market, it ultimately led to allegations of discrimination, sexual harassment, and hostile work environment prior to Kalanick's departure. Uber suffered the largest first-day loss of any business in U.S. history after its IPO in 2019. (Ungarino) The company revamped itself during the 2020 pandemic by leveraging Uber Eats, but only after an extensive culture transformation.

Organizational culture can be a formidable obstacle to change. As the late management guru Peter Drucker said, "Culture eats strategy for breakfast." A well-meaning leader, even the CEO of an organization, can develop a provocative vision of where the business should be—but if that direction runs counter to the established organizational culture, it's likely the vision will never be realized.

So, what does this mean for remote leaders? As team members become more distributed, or at least more fluid in how often they will physically meet, remote leaders cannot let the culture become more diluted. Team performance might suffer if the current culture begins to slip away. An even bigger challenge is to create a remote-first environment, a significant change that must align with the culture and incorporate the organization's values if it's going to stick.

Remember that company with the H1N1 case? After the H1N1 pandemic was over, the majority of the company returned to how they operated prior to the outbreak—because doing so maintained the organizational culture. HR reminded everyone of the company's work-from-home policy, and the CEO publicly championed the flexible work arrangement—yet many teams and departments were still skeptical because of the company's history of requiring in-person presence. They couldn't overcome the culture enough to capitalize on what they had learned during the crisis.

Unfortunately, many companies will go through a similar experience after COVID-19 is behind us. Some organizations that were forced to send workers home will be quick to call their team members back to the workplace. Their organizational culture will prevent them from leveraging the experience and using the lessons learned to find better ways of doing business.

Leaders that want to change their culture to adopt remote working, or those that are concerned with how to maintain their existing culture when everyone is dispersed, must first understand how culture is established.

> **Understand the culture before trying to change the strategy.**

BUILDING AN ORGANIZATIONAL CULTURE

Organizational culture is a collection of beliefs, values, assumptions, experiences, and attitudes that is developed by the organization's members. Initially, the culture might reflect the beliefs and attitudes of the founders or early managers. As the organization grows and adds new people, newly hired leaders and team members contribute to the culture's evolution. This is one reason selecting the right candidates (Chapter 4) is so important. Smart leaders help maintain the culture by consistently choosing new leaders and team members whose values align with the organization.

Online shoe and clothing retailer Zappos is an example of a business that takes "culture fit" seriously. Their human resources staff interviews all candidates to evaluate how well the applicant will fit the culture, and that interview makes up half the determination of whether the candidate is hired. This makes the hiring process relatively slow, with multiple rounds of interviews. Candidates might be asked to attend a company meeting so Zappos employees not involved in the interview process can meet the applicant and provide their feedback. (Heathfield)

Each new Zappos hire goes through four weeks of onboarding that includes culture training. At the end of the four weeks, Zappos makes an unusual offer: They will pay new hires for their time spent in training plus an additional $2,000 bonus to quit, right then and there. No more than 3 percent of the new hires take the deal. (MacFarland)

Why? Zappos does such an effective job selecting the right candidates that management can confidently make the offer without fear of writing lots of checks.

Ironically, Zappos was not a big fan of remote working prior to the COIVD-19 pandemic. Back in 2013, CEO Tony Hsieh said, "We don't really telecommute at Zappos. We want employees to be interacting with each other, building those personal relationships and relationships outside of work as well." (Business Insider)

However, over the years, Zappos has become more remote-friendly as it has embraced a decentralized governance model known as *holacracy*, which allows teams to be much more self-managed. Teams are empowered to decide if they want to work from home, occasionally or full-time.

When the pandemic struck and employees were sent home, many of Zappos' teams quickly pivoted and embraced remote work. Corporate leaders decided to keep the office closed until 2021. They now report that many employees want to shift to a hybrid remote model when the offices finally open. (Vasel)

How strong is your organization's culture? Are you so confident in your hiring process that you would make the same offer to new hires that Zappos does? If not, why not? What would it take to strengthen the recruiting and selection process? Now, think about how this would need to change if your organization were shifting to a remote or fluid hybrid working model.

> **Make sure you bring people into the organization that fit the culture.**

In Chapter 4, we listed some competencies to look for when hiring remote or hybrid team members. You'll want to add to that list with the attributes found in your organization's culture that you want to see reflected in your associates. For example, if your organizational culture values innovation and risk-taking, ask your candidates how they have demonstrated that behavior in the past. Listen for examples of when the candidate innovated or took a chance while they weren't face-to-face with peers or supervisors.

Once a new hire has been brought onboard, how well they adapt and maintain the culture is largely up to the leader. Leaders at all levels ensure that employee behaviors align with the culture. In fact, direct managers and supervisors have more influence than leaders further up the hierarchy. The CEO might publish the vision, mission, and values of the organization, but team members will ultimately behave according to the day-to-day direction they get from their immediate manager.

Leaders are role models and should consciously make decisions about their own behavior that will exemplify the conduct they want their team members to demonstrate. This is especially important when new team members join a remote or hybrid team. New members are absorbing and observing everything around them to better understand expectations and how the team works together. Positive modeling of desired behaviors can be as simple as ensuring the video is turned on during videoconferences or not texting paragraphs of information that would be better conveyed in an email or a meeting. It can also be more complex, such as appropriately demonstrating how to collaborate remotely.

In some regards, it might be easier if the entire team works remotely. When the leader also works remotely, there's greater awareness of the difficulties and success strategies for remote work. It becomes more challenging in a fluid hybrid team with some members remote and some on-site—and with a changing mix of each. The leader may demonstrate behaviors of those who work on-site but forget to proactively reinforce these behaviors with the remote realm.

> Leaders should "walk the talk" by working remotely to better understand what their team experiences.

Remote team members may feel disenfranchised if leaders are not leading by example. If the leader has a permanent on-site office, the leader should occasionally (if not frequently) also work remotely so the leader experiences the same benefits and challenges team members face when working remotely.

MAINTAINING A CULTURE OF PERFORMANCE

Why do some managers fear letting their teams work remotely? Many we spoke with believed their strong organizational culture would erode if team members weren't physically present. But physical separation shouldn't kill the culture if leaders take active measures to keep the team operating within the accepted norms and stated values of the organization. To borrow an old adage, "It's not *what* you do, but *how* you do it." The *how* refers to behavior governed by the organization's culture.

It might seem like a paradox, but the leader's first priority should be to preserve the *what*. Focusing on maintaining expected performance levels will help keep everyone engaged and mitigate the slow drift away from established norms.

In the spring of 2020, when the U.S. implemented mandatory quarantines and organizations were forced to send millions of workers home, some employees struggled with the change. In some cases, these workers also had children learning from home and spouses or partners working from home. The challenges of balancing work and home life were significant. Productivity seemed to slow down.

The situation in 2020 was extreme because of the suddenness of the epidemic and the fear that accompanied it. Business operations did slow down as everyone learned to adjust and adapt to working remotely. In a post-pandemic world, remote and hybrid working should not degrade the business or its culture. In fact, in order to sustain the culture, leaders should demand high performance from their team members, as the following example shows.

> "I've learned to be a lot more patient. I used to get immediate responses to certain questions. Even if I couldn't walk over to someone's cubicle, I could at least get a quick email response. Now, someone is home doing double duty, taking care of their kids, and trying to work. I may not get a response until late in the evening when everything calms down for them."

Jason, one of the authors, served in the Army many years ago. One afternoon at Fort Benning, Georgia, he was having lunch with a Sergeant Major, the senior ranking non-commissioned officer in the unit, along with several other younger soldiers. The Sergeant Major had more than twenty years in uniform. He'd served in a couple of wars and spent most of his career with elite units, such as the famed 75th Ranger Regiment. During lunch, one of the younger soldiers asked, "Sergeant Major, how do you create a unit with high morale?"

The soldier was essentially asking how to create a team that would be highly motivated or have a positive culture. We all waited eagerly for the response, as though we were about to hear an answer from an oracle. The Sergeant Major thought for several moments before responding.

"Honestly, I don't know," he finally said. "But I can tell you this: In every unit that I ever served in that had high morale, from the Rangers to the 82nd Airborne, they were also high performing. I don't think they were high-performing organizations because they had high morale. I think it was the other way around. I think they had high morale because they had high performance. Therefore, always focus on being the best at what you do. Performance creates momentum that impacts the attitudes of the team members, which in turn helps to create even higher performance."

We can use this as a lesson about performance and culture. It may seem like a chicken-and-egg argument: Does a strong, positive organizational culture result in high performance or does performing well help build the culture? We believe that culture doesn't have to precede performance, but holding employees accountable to performance measures that reflect the culture is absolutely necessary to preserve it. For example, if an organization has an outcome-oriented culture, leaders will need to create a sense of urgency about achieving key performance indicators. If the culture is customer-centric, leaders should push their team members to find ways to make their customers happy. Regardless of workers being remote or on-site, all team members need to achieve performance targets while exhibiting expected behavior and values.

> **Don't know where to start? Identify what's important and set high performance expectations.**

THE LEADER'S TOOLKIT FOR PRESERVING AND STRENGTHENING THE CULTURE

Let's assume that some leaders have a strong, positive organizational culture that propels business performance, and they don't want to lose this culture as they move from a remote-friendly to remote-first environment. Other leaders might already have a hybrid or remote model, and they want to strengthen or build a strong culture that will bind employees together as they progress toward their shared goals.

Besides exercising good leadership, role modeling behaviors, and relentlessly pursuing high performance, what else can leaders do to preserve and strengthen their culture? Here are a few tactics.

Use the Culture Buddy System

Leaders may have the biggest influence on the organization's culture, but the second biggest influence are the employees in the organization. As Mike Smith, former Atlanta Falcons football coach, once said, "Culture is defined and created from the top down, but it comes to life from the bottom up." Peers can help reinforce the "right" set of behaviors and discourage the "wrong" ones. Leaders can engage peer groups through buddy systems or social networks.

The San Francisco-based finance company Landed assigns a "culture buddy" to all new hires. (Dill) Unlike a mentor, the culture buddy is not there to necessarily teach the new hire how to do his job or develop her for future promotions. Instead, the culture buddy is there as a go-to resource for any questions about team or company *norms*. If a new hire has a question about appropriate virtual meeting etiquette, they go to their culture buddy. If they want to know when it is more desirable to be in the office versus being remote, the culture buddy is available to give advice.

Creating a buddy system can also help team members stay engaged and connected. Analytics and survey giant Gallup includes a question in their employee engagement survey that asks if an associate has a best friend at work. Gallup found a correlation between employees who had a best friend and increased engagement, reduced turnover, and yes, even higher profits. The logic behind the question is that when we have strong ties with team members or other colleagues within the organization, we are more likely to apply additional, discretionary effort to benefit the organization. (Mann)

> Peer groups can encourage the right behaviors and discourage the wrong

Of course, assigning a culture buddy to a new team member doesn't guarantee those two will become best friends and produce the results that Gallup found—but it does give the new hire a place to start. Newly hired remote workers, and hybrid team members to some degree, can find it difficult to create bonds because they have fewer opportunities to meet others in the organization. Virtual teams can be more task-focused when they meet and not take time for social interactions. It might be up to the leader to give new team members their first social contact within the organization. The buddy system is one tool you can use.

Create a Social Network

Ideally, all team members will become part of an intra-organizational "social network" of relationships. Leaders can help new members create additional social ties within the organization and strengthen existing ones. Team members not located with the critical mass of workers might not have the opportunity to meet others outside of their direct team. They might hear the names of, but never have met, some of the other leaders in the organization— even months after they're hired.

Leaders can help facilitate introductions and do a "warm handoff," by formally introducing the new member to specific people, so remote team members get to know others. Simply reserving time in meetings for social interactions can also help. Once strong bonds form between team members, they are more likely to transfer knowledge and reinforce behaviors that will maintain the culture.

Find or Create Rituals and Culture Habits

You might be reading through the examples of the buddy system or social networks and thinking it only applies to new hires. But bonds can form and be reinforced among employees who have already become oriented to the organization, too.

Leaders can leverage the various company rituals—the consistent, repetitive sequence of activities that team members participate in—to reinforce the culture across their entire team. Organizational life is filled with rituals, from quarterly business meetings to weekly staff meetings to the annual holiday party. Smaller rituals appear more as culture habits, such as how a team solves a problem, responds to a customer's need, or celebrates success.

One outbound marketing call center we know used to have all of their agents working together in a call center. When an agent made a sale, the agent or their supervisor would ring a bell that was heard across the floor. Other agents would cheer at the sound. Now, all the company's agents work from home. To *replicate* the enthusiasm generated in the office, the new ritual is to announce new sales over group chat. This allows other agents to offer praise with emoticons and words of encouragement.

Culture habits—the *how* things get done—should be thought through. If the organizational culture stresses collaboration, how should team members collaborate when several team members are remote? If the team members who work together in the same office hold meetings but don't make efforts to include and solicit participation from the virtual team members, the collaborative culture will dissolve. Collaboration must include at least giving everyone a chance to participate.

In a team-oriented culture, the leader might rotate the time of their weekly meeting to accommodate team members in different time zones. These small acts can contribute, over time, to the nurturing or neglect of the organization's culture.

Make it a Game

Over the past decade, *gamification*—using game elements in non-game contexts—has become popular in marketing. Hotels and airlines reward frequent customers with points, and even Starbucks offers a reward app that fills your virtual cup with bonus stars for every purchase. Gamification has also proven useful to motivate employees by displaying visible leaderboards or awarding badges or other symbols based on performance. It can also be used to reinforce the organizational culture. Earlier in the chapter, we described the strong culture at Zappos. Zappos employees can earn points for various activities, such as being the first person on the team to send a good morning message. Employees who accumulate enough points can exchange them for swag items. (Christoffersen) This unlocks the competitive spirit within team members while rewarding them for behaviors that are aligned to cultural values.

Rather than handing down mandates or explaining how team members should act, leaders can determine specific, tangible actions they want team members to perform and make it fun. The key is to make team members want to perform versus feeling that they are forced to behave in a certain way.

Continually Reassess

Change is inevitable. Leaders should never be afraid to revisit their published values and norms from time to time to be sure they still match the organization's reality. Knowing what's working and what's not working will help leaders recalibrate. They might need to reinforce or sustain the culture—or correct their course.

Leaders at all levels, and even individual contributors with no direct reports, can influence the direction of the team or organization. All team members—whether they are in the physical workplace fulltime, are typically remote, or function within a fluid hybrid team structure—should be encouraged to provide their feedback on how team functioning aligns with cultural values.

The COVID-19 pandemic disrupted most business operations, and many things had to change. But disruption can bring about positive changes if you use it as an opportunity to reexamine how things are done and choose the best ways to move forward.

7

COLLABORATING AND INNOVATING IN THE VIRTUAL WORKPLACE

Have you ever heard of Luther Haws? If you haven't, that's a shame, because Luther Haws invented collaboration and innovation.

Haws was an American inventor. While working as a sanitary inspector for the city of Berkley, California, in 1905, Haws had a revolutionary idea. His idea was what we now know as the water cooler. Sure, it would be another seventy-five years before the huge glass jugs were replaced with plastic ones, eventually making it easier to transport and a staple of the modern office—but where would companies be without the indispensable water dispenser? Where would employees congregate, exchange ideas, and have spontaneous conversations that would lead to the next big thing?

We admit we are being a little facetious. Organizations put too much stock in the so-called "water cooler conversations." For example, according to Walter Isaacson's biography of Steve Jobs, when Pixar's headquarters was built in 1999, Jobs wanted his staff of artists, writers, and computer scientists to be in constant contact with each other. Employee mailboxes, meeting rooms, cafeteria, coffee bar, gift shop, and even restrooms were moved to the center of the building. Did it make a difference? It's hard to argue with the genius of Steve Jobs, but we remain skeptical of the impact of the much-touted hallway conversations and impromptu drop-ins that occur in a traditional office environment.

Mr. Haws' invention is back in the news today, as a concern of remote leaders. Don't spontaneous exchanges lead to new ideas or solutions? Is the organization losing innovative ideas or its competitive edge if people are dispersed through cyber space and can't gather on-site?

The answer is no. Of course, face-to-face interactions are valuable and contribute to a number of positive team dynamics. Face-to-face is great—when it's possible. But in-person meetings are usually not *necessary*. We have yet to meet (or even hear about) the group of employees who solved the organization's complex dilemma or invented the company's new cash-cow product while waiting for their lunch to heat up in the breakroom microwave.

> **Collaboration and innovation are not dependent on physical proximity.**

In reality, new ideas or solutions to complicated problems are usually developed by teams over time, as they focus on a particular area. Most people have experienced this in face-to-face encounters, both formal and informal, and that makes them more comfortable with collaboration when everyone is in the same room. But we're beginning to see that handling everything on-site is not essential.

So why does the water cooler myth—and all that it connotes—prevail? Why do most people believe that collaboration must happen face-to-face? Why is it that the word "collaborate" conjures visions of a team huddled around a whiteboard?

Our interviewees and survey respondents often said this:

"The biggest challenge to working remotely is brainstorming and whiteboarding."

"It's so much more effective to collaborate in-person."

"People are social animals. We need to be physically together to come up with new ideas."

Do you still believe that? Does your brain default to the myth that we have to be looking into someone else's eyes when we have a great idea? Why does this misperception still exist?

It might have something to do with trust and experience. In order for collaboration-at-a-distance to work, leaders and team members need to have:

- Trust and experience (familiarity) within their team and among colleagues (see Chapter 1)

- Trust and experience in the process

- Trust and experience with the tools they are using to collaborate.

In this chapter, we will explore these areas and discuss how to make collaboration, and in turn innovation, work well when people can't meet on-site because they are many miles apart.

TRUSTING THE TEAM

We discussed trust in Chapter 1 and communication in Chapter 2 as the foundational principles of remote and hybrid teams. Without trust and good communication, there can be no effective collaboration. A team leader can employ many strategies to increase both trust and communication within the virtual team. Specifically, the more there is an increase in social identity from a distance and interaction among team members, the more this will fuel engagement—which is where collaboration begins.

> For effective collaboration, team members need to feel that they are part of the team.

Social identity theory, which has been around for nearly half a century, explains that we all find ways to identify with various groups. The more we identify with a group, the more likely we will behave in a manner consistent with the interests of the group, putting our own needs and desires aside. (Tajfel and Turner) Greater identification with a dispersed group can lead to greater trust and cohesion, better communication and cooperation, and ultimately, better performance. (Ellemers, et al.)

It is more challenging to help team members feel that they are part of a remote team. Without being able to see each other—especially when different time zones make even video calls problematic—it's hard to encourage the kind of cohesiveness the leader will need for collaboration.

How can a leader increase social identity within the group? The first step in building a high-performing, collaborative team is to select the right team members.

You might have heard the stages of group development described as *forming, storming, norming, and performing*. You'll find a lot of information about the first stage, forming, in Chapter 4. Although we referred to how individuals are selected and brought into the organization, the same principles apply when choosing members to be part of a team. A leader might want to choose at least some team members based on their experience and past performance working within a virtual team, so they are already comfortable and adept at working virtually.

If it can be arranged, some face-to-face meetings in the early stages of the team's development are ideal. Trust can erode without visual cues in communication. (Box, et al.)

If the team members have all "laid eyes on" each other at least once, the team will have a greater foundation for trust. It's best to create an opportunity for everyone to be present at the initiation of a new team. The leader will need to work through logistical and budgetary constraints to bring team members face-to-face when possible.

> **Try to select team members that are skilled or experienced in working remotely.**

For a new team, an initial on-site kickoff meeting can help foster closer interpersonal relationships. But we can't always make that happen. If a leader understands the key components of remote team effectiveness and takes appropriate actions to reinforce these as the team is forming or as new members join, the leader will be able to have a successful team without on-site meetings.

> **"We sometimes have meetings where no work is discussed. It keeps us connected and makes us realize that we are all going through the same experience. I feel closer to my co-workers because of this."**

Don't forget to make time for social interactions. When a virtual team meets, they're likely to roll up their sleeves and get to work—which leaves little time for social chit chat—yet that small talk can lead to big dividends in helping team members feel that they belong together.

Virtual relationships take time, multiple interactions, and shared experiences to grow. Social communication helps improve trust among team members (see Chapter 2), which is vital for collaboration.

When teams collaborate brilliantly on a concept, it's not because they have come into physical contact with one another often—it's because team members trust one another and feel comfortable sharing their ideas.

TRUSTING THE PROCESS

Not long ago, we participated in a company brainstorming session to develop a new way for customers to get faster and more accurate information about their orders. The meeting organizer sent a digital invitation to a cross-functional group that included three remote participants and about ten team members who would be on-site in the meeting room. The only clue about the topic of the meeting was in the subject line of the invitation; the meeting agenda was not included.

When the meeting began, the meeting organizer greeted everyone and took a quick roll call—including the three people who introduced themselves from the teleconference unit sitting in the middle of the conference table—and then walked up to the dry-erase board and stated the problem the group was to solve.

She then provided the brainstorming ground rules—participants could shout out any idea, no idea was a bad idea, no one would criticize an idea, and no idea was too wild or too crazy. The goal was to generate as many ideas as possible. "Okay," she said, "you can start throwing out those ideas now!"

A long, awkward silence followed.

> **Innovation is a process – one that requires structure.**

Have you ever been through a similar scenario? How hard is it to be the first one to suggest an idea in this situation?

If we put creative people into a room, good ideas will come forth, right? Unfortunately, research has shown this is not the case. Groups that follow the traditional guidelines for brainstorming or problem-solving generate fewer ideas than individuals alone. (Mullen, et al) In a group, ideas start to converge, and the diversity of thought is lost. (Markman)

When team members are given a blank sheet of paper or a blank white board and told to be creative, creativity often freezes.

Research has produced specific problem-solving methods, like PDCA, 8D, Lean, and Six Sigma, which provide step-by-step methodology. The concept there is that, to collaborate better and develop creative solutions or ideas, we often need *more* structure and not less.

In Chapter 3, we described the small experiment conducted at Frostburg State University in which people had to pick up a ball from the table in order to speak and then replace it when they were finished. Researchers found that adding even this small amount of structure to how participants interacted made their communication much more effective. Participants said, after the exercise, that holding the "talking ball" empowered them.

Trusting the process can be as simple as working with an existing structure and sticking to it. The leader must consider how to incorporate remote participants, to ensure their contributions are included. In the "failed brainstorming" scenario at the beginning of this section, three remote participants were on the phone, but not on video. The remote team members couldn't even see the ideas the facilitator was writing on the white board. How could she have made this work better?

Perhaps the facilitator could have used video or the screen-sharing functionality in a meeting app to share a virtual white board. She might also have used a "breakout room" function and let all participants work in small groups to generate ideas before sharing them with the full team. Even with the limitations of teleconference technology, the facilitator could have asked everyone to prepare some ideas in advance, individually, and then present their ideas to the group. Any of these ideas would have improved the collaboration between on-site and remote team members, making the meeting more productive and a more satisfying hybrid team experience.

Ideally, collaboration won't always have to depend on technology. When a leader has team members who are comfortable working with each other and with the leader, the structure will matter much less. The team will bring about great ideas and solutions, regardless of where the members are located. But while everyone is adapting to working remotely, it's important for leaders to do what they can to build trust and enhance communication.

The right tools will help a leader make this process even more interactive and engaging.

TRUST & MASTER THE TOOLS

Imagine you are assigned to a new team that is responsible for developing a new idea that leverages your company's flagship product. All of your team members are remote, and your only means of communication is via email.

If you cringe at that thought, you are not alone. But it wasn't that many years ago when email and phone calls were the only real means for remote teams to communicate. Think about this: the term "telecommute" was coined a few years before the first fax machines appeared in the workplace! Thankfully, we have much better tools and technology available to teams today, and they continue to improve.

The exponential speed at which technology evolves makes it difficult to offer recommendations for any specific technology solution, platform, or app. It's entirely possible that between the time we are writing this and when you are reading, new products will emerge on the market. Some will replace currently popular platforms, while others will be introduced and abandoned in short order.

We will outline the basic tools found today in almost every popular meeting application to make collaboration more effective. These functions will likely continue to be used in the near future.

❖ **Video.** Video makes an important difference when teams collaborate. Studies have shown that team members feel better about the quality of their interactions as the quality of video increases. (Burke and Chidambaram) Years ago, low-quality web cams made users look pixelated and delayed their responses (or worse – "froze" them in unflattering facial expressions). High-quality videoconferencing has resolved most of these issues. If the team is fortunate enough to have access to higher-end videoconferencing, the leader should encourage its use. It's easier for people to collaborate when they can clearly observe non-verbal cues and body language, have high-quality audio connections, and enjoy reliable video connectivity.

> "Collaboration suffered in the beginning. With some modification of meeting schedules, using video rather than just audio, and being very transparent when things are challenging, we have been able to get back the great environment we had when we were in the office together."

❖ **Screen sharing and multi-share.** By now, most remote leaders and distance teams are well aware of the importance of using the screen-sharing tool when visual information is required, for demonstrations or presentations. As a tip, rotate screen sharing between participants to increase engagement. Most applications also have a multi-share to allow more than one person to share simultaneously. Use this when comparing ideas or documents.

❖ **Chat.** Why would meeting participants need this functionality when they can use instant messaging? Using chat within the meeting app allows everyone to see the question and its answer or share a related comment. Participants can download a transcript of the chat at the end of the meeting, so they don't have to take notes. As mentioned in Chapter 3 on meetings, if a meeting leader is using group chat, it's helpful to have someone else manage the chat, collecting or answering questions that are raised.

❖ **Raise hand, use emoticons.** The meeting leader can ask participants to virtually raise their hands (as we described in Chapter 3) or use an emoticon to quickly gauge how everyone is doing and to keep them engaged. Doing a quick check with emoticons is a simple way to see how participants are reacting to the discussion.

❖ **Annotation and whiteboarding.** When leading a virtual meeting, the traditional "whiteboard" is usually available in the online meeting platform. Drawing with a mouse might feel clunky at first, but it gets easier with practice. Using a stylus on a touch screen is even easier. Most virtual meeting platforms also offer annotation, which lets participants draw on the screen, use text, create shapes, highlight, and point out items of interest. Leaders should encourage the team to practice using these features and master them themselves. Virtual team members will be more engaged if they can be "hands-on" during the meeting, rather than just watching a "talking-head" facilitator. And remember, a plethora of new virtual meeting functions are continually being developed.

❖ **Remote control.** Do you need to co-edit a document in real time? Some video conferencing platforms will allow a remote meeting member to take control of another participant's screen, using a remote-control feature. Then two or more people can have input at the same time.

❖ **Breakout rooms.** Have you ever been in a meeting where so many participants wanted to speak at the same time that little was accomplished? The logistics of breaking the participants into smaller groups and sending them to separate areas to work out their ideas would seem challenging and time-consuming. (Imagine all the sighing and squeaking chairs and resentful muttering as people were asked to stand and walk to another spot, and then return.) But dividing virtual meeting attendees into smaller groups is so easy! The meeting leader can ask team members to work on specific issues or pieces of a larger problem and then rejoin a larger group to share answers.

Tools of the not-so-distant future are likely to support collaboration in even more effective and engaging ways. Leaders might soon be using augmented and virtual reality or holographic images. But no matter what develops, remote leaders still need to commit to becoming proficient with the tools by experimenting, learning, and mastering these resources and encouraging their teams to do the same.

REMOTE WORK AS THE CATALYST FOR INNOVATING IN THE ENTERPRISE

Organizations implement remote work programs for various reasons, from saving real-estate costs to improving employee satisfaction—and the 2020 pandemic or another national crisis can be a powerful motivator. We've explored the challenges and difficulties team leaders might face once team members are dispersed or working from home—but haven't really looked at the huge opportunity to innovate remote work provides. Incorporating a team that is scattered geographically will likely cause a leader to study the way things in the organization are done and might prompt a search for ways to do them better.

> **Use remote working as an opportunity to re-examine HOW works gets done.**

Learning to manage a remote team will help leaders become more comfortable with considering the talent pool outside of the local geographic area. If the organization is located in a rural, agriculture-dominant area, and a leader is looking for employees with extensive experience in Python, it might make sense to consider applicants from Silicon Valley to Bangalore. Or there may be benefit to a "follow the sun" strategy in which team members are intentionally dispersed around the globe for twenty-four/seven workflow or service support. But learning to lead remotely can provide additional opportunities to improve internal processes, as well.

About a decade ago, we were asked to consult with a bank that had recently implemented a policy to let associates work from home a few days a week. But they encountered a problem. Their loan processing protocol required seven physical signatures on the document before it could be finalized. How could their at-home workers manage this? The manager's first thought was to ask everyone to come in on a specific day—a *signing day*—so the required people would be physically present to sign their names.

"Why do you need seven signatures?" we asked. Was it a regulatory requirement? Wasn't there a way to streamline the number of bureaucratic levels the paperwork had to pass through? Did all signatures have to be physical, or might electronic signatures work? (At that time, electronic signature capability was fairly new and not widely used.) We encouraged the manager to step back and reconsider the entire process.

Perhaps unsurprisingly, leaders at the bank didn't see the implementation of remote work as an opportunity to re-examine how they do business. They could only see the immediate challenges remote working caused. Leaders should always ask if there is a better way to do things. The current pandemic has made many businesses review their processes, because "how we've always done it" just might not be possible now.

Another organization we know well, a multi-site car dealership, understood this concept. Anyone who has purchased a car at a dealership is probably familiar with the multi-level process. You browse cars, take a test drive, and negotiate a deal. Assuming you've reached an agreement with the sales rep, you are usually handed off to a finance manager to review and sign all the paperwork before you can drive off the lot with your newly purchased automobile. This closing process can take an hour or more, in addition to all the time you spent looking at and test-driving vehicles and haggling with the salesperson. It's no wonder that most people dread the car buying experience.

For the car dealership we studied, the closing process was the bottleneck. On the weekends, when there was a high volume of customers, the finance department would get overwhelmed. Customers were forced to sit in the lobby to wait for the next available finance manager, giving them a chance to reconsider and walk out of the showroom. The COVID-19 pandemic meant the dealership had to put in a number of safety precautions, which only seemed to add more time to the process.

However, the owner of the dealership recognized an opportunity. What if the closing process could be done remotely? He owned several dealerships, and each had a couple of finance managers; what if closings could be centralized, so that any available finance manager could handle the next customer in the queue? They were already using electronic devices to capture e-signatures.

They installed video in the closing rooms, and the next available finance managers would remotely walk the customer through the closing steps and electronically collect the required signatures to close the sale. This innovation not only sped up the process for customers, but it lowered the risk of contagion.

Obviously, implementing this kind of change is no simple task. They had to standardize processes, install equipment, and train the staff. But the leaders at the dealership knew that less time waiting would translate to a better customer experience, and in the long run, they'd save money by needing fewer finance managers in total.

Innovating isn't easy. The pandemic was the tipping point for the car dealership, forcing them to seek a better way. Imagine how long it might have taken them to change their process if they weren't forced to adapt. Imagine how many dealerships are still closing sales the old way.

Enabling team members to work remotely, even in a fluid hybrid model, can be a catalyst for much broader change. The basic premise is still the same: Get the right team together, follow a structured process, and master the tools that facilitate collaboration. Then take a look at how things can be done better. Leaders might find that remote work can produce meaningful, long-lasting changes that take the organization to new heights.

8

ADDRESSING REMOTE TEAM CHALLENGES

An extraordinary national crisis like the COVID-19 pandemic impacts many aspects of remote work. After decades of consulting with organizations and training thousands of people on the "right" way to work remotely, we were more than a little stunned to watch how many of those guidelines were necessarily abandoned in 2020 as businesses scrambled to accommodate the new situation.

Any time the workforce shifts to remote work in response to an emergency—like a hurricane, tornado, terrorism, infrastructure failure, flood, fire, etc.—leaders and teams face unpredictable situations. Effective business continuity planning can mitigate some of the factors that might compromise workflow, but other factors will be difficult to anticipate. The worldwide pandemic and resulting lockdown of 2020 is a glaring example of this "who could have imagined?" dynamic.

Businesses we interviewed and surveyed described problems for which they had no solutions. They had been inadequately prepared for the sudden closure of many traditional work sites. Resources were a big issue. Many people were more dependent than they realized on specific equipment, tools, and technology resources that didn't go home with them. Some organizations had difficulty hosting virtual meetings. Some faced network and data security issues because their technology infrastructure was weak.

Many workers also faced overwhelming personal challenges, trying to work with children and other family members also trying to work from home. They were afraid of the illness and didn't know how long the lockdown might last. It became nearly impossible to balance work and family demands, focus on work, and feel that everything was manageable.

So, what did we learn from this unplanned and phenomenally intense fast-track to remote working?

A few key insights became clear as the pandemic dragged on, workplaces remain closed, schools struggled to open with a safe environment. We were able to contrast planned remote work with remote work prompted by an emergency. We offer these observations:

- Organizations that had previously embraced or at least partially implemented remote work were better able to adapt.

- Many leaders were pleasantly surprised by how effectively work could be accomplished during the tended work-from-home experience.

- Team members were patient and tolerant, for the most part. There was an overall sense of acceptance of children appearing on camera, bad hair days, casual dress, barking dogs, and noisy backgrounds. It was sometimes impossible to maintain a standard of decorum that existed pre-pandemic, and workers learned to overlook and forgive that.

- Comfort levels with video meetings really zoomed (pun intended!). The value of connecting by video became apparent, as people increasingly recognized the risks of isolation and the value of "seeing" each other for work and personal connectivity. Those who were already skilled at using video tools adapted more easily.

- People became creative about ways to replicate and simulate some of the interpersonal experiences they missed by not being together. They found ways to have fun and retain important bonds of communication, sharing, and support.

- Certain tasks—such as sales prospecting, performance reviews, and problem-solving—were initially pushed back. But when it became clear that remote work would continue for far longer than originally expected, teams found ways to tackle those chores—because further delaying them would have hurt business.

- Teams and leaders who made concerted efforts to reach out to each other in a variety of ways were less frustrated by the impact of the extended remote work time. Those who specifically connected at a personal (not just task) level reported feeling more engaged with their team and leader.

- Digital overload resulting from so many video meetings became a problem as work-from-home was extended. People realized that it was difficult to stare at a video screen for the same number of minutes it would take to hold an in-person meeting. Video meeting burn-out became an increasing complaint.

- Leaders felt the stress, frustration, and exhaustion of team members as the pandemic wore on. Many responded by ramping up coaching, support, and additional virtual touch points with team members. They tried to foster optimism, even as employees were furloughed and departments were shut down and businesses folded. Leaders found that openness, transparency, and increased communication was vital to helping people survive this process.

Although the pandemic created extraordinary and unpredicted circumstances, leaders and team members who worked together and learned to adapt created solutions to some of the most vexing problems of the virtual workplace. Some leaders gained valuable experience in overcoming (or managing) remote work obstacles.

DIGITAL OVERLOAD IN THE HYPER-CONNECTED WORKPLACE

In 2020, video burnout became a thing. Many team members reported that they were communicating with their leader and their peers more than ever before, but some felt they were in touch too frequently. All agreed they were spending too many hours on the computer.

Although communication is the solution to many problems, some people felt exhausted from being on one video meeting after another. Some failed to master the multiple tools that might have made their jobs easier.

> **IN OUR EXPERIENCE...**
>
> *An employee for a mid-size logistics company told us that his company provided employees with three video meeting platforms. "I never know which one to use," he told us. "They're all slightly different. I'd spend the first couple of minutes of any meeting just trying to remember how to get into and effectively use the meeting app." When we asked if he knew all the functionality in the various apps, he said "At some point, I stopped trying to learn them all. I just don't have time for this."*

A leader can help the team learn to effectively use meeting platform tools. In Chapter 3, we discussed the importance of setting time aside in meetings for more social interaction before jumping into the tasks or objectives of the meeting. Don't be afraid to get a little creative and try a few fun ways to keep people engaged (see Appendix A for ways to use virtual icebreakers).

Leaders should also keep the following in mind:

❖ **Video meeting maximums:** Limit video meetings to a maximum length, such as three hours. Schedule multiple breaks if a virtual meeting must go past this time limit.

❖ **Not everything has to be done over a video.** Despite the benefits of video meetings, shorter meetings done by phone or teleconference can be a welcome relief to team members with video burnout.

❖ **Set expectations.** Work with the team to create expectations for work hours, response times on emails, and parameters for returning calls. You'll find more information about this in Appendix C.

BURNOUT, ISOLATION, AND FINDING WORK/LIFE BALANCE

Many of the leaders we surveyed agreed that remote team members are just as productive, if not more, than employees working in an office full time. In fact, many cited productivity as a major advantage to remote teams.

Over the past two decades, multiple studies have shown that workers feel more productive when they work remotely. Why? Maybe it's because workers *work more hours*

"Email was bad before, but now with multiple communication platforms (email, Skype, Teams, etc.), I feel like I'm playing whack–a–mole all day with unread notifications."

than their in-office counterparts. A study by Brigham Young University several years ago found that remote workers could log nineteen more hours per week than office-bound workers before feeling that work was interfering with their personal life. People can accomplish a great deal in nineteen extra hours a week.

But is this a good thing for remote team members? Many remote workers told us, "I have a hard time turning everything off." Particularly during the pandemic, remote workers felt compelled to work late in the evening to make up for what they perceived was lost time when they were balancing multiple responsibilities during the daytime.

Some remote employees spent the pandemic quarantines providing childcare, homeschooling, or eldercare—as well as working at their jobs. They reported scrolling through their work email on their smartphones when their shift was over. In a connected virtual workplace, work never seems to never stop.

It was a bigger challenge for the many *instant* remote workers who found themselves suddenly working from home during the pandemic. The extra effort and hours they put in might have been beneficial for their employers, in the short-term—but it might ultimately cost those organizations if their best team members become burned out.

Burned-out workers tend to become apathetic, call off sick more, or even leave their jobs. Be aware of the workloads team members are carrying. Just because leaders can access their associates twenty-four hours a day, that doesn't mean they should. Be aware of unstated norms that team members have to be available all the time. Leaders must get to know team members and their personal challenges. Explore ways to help minimize stress and burnout for everyone on the team.

> **"The biggest surprise was that, as opposed to what I expected, we end up working more from home. And by working more, I mean we actually get more things done and spend more hours working."**

These tips can help employees balance their workloads while working remotely:

❖ **Set priorities.** Perhaps the biggest responsibility of the leader is to set priorities, goals, and accountabilities for the team and ensure every team member knows them. Be clear about where their main focus should be, to reduce the risk they will become distracted by nonessential tasks.

❖ **Establish work practices.** If possible, set work hours and establish rituals by which the workday clearly begins and ends.

❖ **Encourage team members to set up a helpful workspace.** Each remote worker needs to find the right place to work; but because productivity depends on it, leaders can become involved, too. Think about the difference between working from the living room coffee table and working from a home office space. Encourage team members to find a space that can be clearly delineated from their living space.

❖ **Encourage team members to be healthy.** It's not often that a boss tells his or her employee to take a break. But a healthy team member is a productive and high-performing team member, and health is dependent on getting enough rest and "down time." Help the team identify ways to reduce stress and stay healthy, such as exercise, relaxation, hobbies, meditation, or walking.

IN OUR EXPERIENCE...

We spoke with a manager working remotely for a global technology company about how he manages his day.

"I have employees in Silicon Valley, three hours behind me; in Europe, six hours ahead of me; and in India, which is ten and a half hours ahead. I quickly realized when I started working in this role that, if I tried to keep up with all my employees, I would end up working twenty-four hours a day. I set my work hours, but I realize that sometimes I have to be available late at night or very, very early in the morning. To make sure I don't work myself to death, I block off time every day to exercise and I occasionally block time off just so I can have a mental health break for thirty minutes to clear my head. I find that the short breaks do wonders for keeping me relaxed and invigorated, so I never get burned out."

Team members, more than leaders, mentioned feelings of isolation as one of their top challenges. Often, they mentioned isolation in the same sentence as having a poor work/life balance. It might be no surprise that team members feel more isolated when they work more hours remotely.

Many of the people that we spoke with or surveyed expressed their longing for personal interactions. Interestingly, they didn't want to work physically together with peers or leaders all the time; but having absolutely no face-to-face contact with colleagues for extended periods made them lonely.

Team members can deal with isolation in a few ways:

- ❖ **Stay in contact.** In Chapter 2, we discussed the importance of the "how goes it" calls and periodic virtual lunch, coffee, or exercise breaks with team members.

- ❖ **Build the social network.** In Chapter 6, we mentioned the power of buddy systems and social networks in the context of maintaining organizational culture. These same systems can also be used to help keep team members engaged and to fight isolation.

- ❖ **Go beyond the team.** Encourage team members to seek opportunities for involvement in projects beyond their immediate job and team, to help grow their social network.

- ❖ **Go beyond the organization.** Ask team members to think about expanding their skills and knowledge by enrolling in classes or seminars, networking through local business associations, joining industry and professional associations, or volunteering for a service association or charity in their community. Remember the team member's workload and personal obligations and be careful not to overload them.

ENSURING WORK–FROM–ANYWHERE EFFECTIVENESS

Not every employee finds it easy to transition to working-from-home. Office dwellers often think of the time they'd save by eliminating their commute, but they might be overly optimistic about their own ability to work remotely. Some new remote workers struggle to maintain focus when surrounded by distractions. Leaders can help them get past this challenge in several ways:

❖ **Ask team members for their Top 3.** We mentioned in Chapter 5 the importance of setting goals and expectations. Long-term goals are valuable, but they allow some people to procrastinate or to get sidetracked by immediate personal issues. Ask team members to list their top 3 priorities for the day or week. Ideally, all priorities will link directly to longer-term goals—but addressing closer goals can help create a sense of urgency to get things done. If they have trouble thinking of their work in terms of priorities, leaders should offer feedback and assistance until they get the hang of it—especially if leaders feel their team members might be focusing on the wrong things.

❖ **Break work down into bite-size pieces.** Similar to the point above, organize work into manageable chunks that can be accomplished in reasonable periods of time. Establish major milestones or deliverables with deadlines, but also set interim deadlines for progress if needed.

❖ **Make it visible.** There's an old adage that what gets measured, gets done. We would add that what gets published publicly is highly likely to get done. Document team goals and make sure everyone can see the progress toward those goals. A little social pressure can help team members stay focused on their established goals.

❖ **Identify the sources of distractions even before they become distractions.** Help team members recognize potential distractions, such as household chores, the needs of family members, pets, personal tasks, web surfing, television, eating/snacking, etc. Then help them develop action plans to manage the distractions.

❖ **Plan for the personal stuff.** Personal issues do come up, but they don't have to interfere with work activities. The leader should ask team members to anticipate the things that might come up and notify the leader (for example, a sudden childcare issue that will require the team member to leave mid-afternoon for a few days in a row to pick up a child and return home). Help them build time in their daily schedule to handle personal needs, so they won't interrupt important work-related activities.

❖ **Recognize and reward.** Establish short-term team goals and provide incentives or rewards. A reward might be a personal message noting the goal achievement or a more public acknowledgement when team members reach or exceed expected targets. Showing team members that their efforts are appreciated is a proven motivator.

BALANCING WORK–LIFE AND FAMILY–LIFE

We would be remiss if we didn't acknowledge the special remote working circumstances the COVID-19 pandemic created. Prior to the pandemic, many remote workers had the luxury of being the only family member at home during business hours. However, the extraordinary events of 2020 forced remote workers to adapt to a new set of distractions. Many remote workers suddenly found

> "Living [and working] in close proximity is stressful and it seemed like we were running a bed & breakfast."

themselves working from home while their spouse or partner was also in the same situation and their children were also learning from home. While this might not always be the case, some remote workers will have family situations that will impact their remote work circumstances and challenges.

To help remote workers manage distractions when multiple family members are home, we recommend negotiating a family agreement to the virtual work arrangement. Remote workers will need to convince their family members of the importance of allowing them to work. The family agreement might include:

- Work hours—What they are and when there might be flexibility

- Interruptions—How to handle them and what can justify them

- Workspace—Where it is and what access others may have to it

- Household chores—Who does what and when

- Childcare—Who is responsible for what and when

Ask team members to talk to their families and secure agreements by having a specific discussion that addresses issues, concerns, fears, or feelings. Similar to a business agreement, the family agreement should be a mutually workable solution, and family members should revisit it often to confirm that it's working. When a conflict or disagreement arises, family members should discuss and proactively resolve it.

Leaders can't control what occurs in their team members' households, but leaders can offer empathy, support, encouragement, and understanding. Proactively discussing supportive ideas and creative solutions to common problems can be helpful. Team leaders can share best practices within the team to overcome situational challenges.

Additionally, leaders can help the team by being patient about distractions, noise, and team meeting drop-in visits by children, pets, and spouses.

MANAGING WORK–FROM–HOME PRODUCTIVITY

We talked before about how setting up a dedicated home workspace can help remote workers maintain their work/life balance. Having such a space also will help them manage distractions, stay focused, and become more productive.

The home workspace needs to be comfortable, safe, and conducive to the activities the team member routinely performs. Leaders can offer the following guidelines to team members for creating a suitable home workspace.

❖ **Find the perfect spot.** Determine how much space is needed and choose a location in the home that will offer at least some privacy and appropriate separation from home or family distractions. Make sure the location is as comfortable and safe as possible, and then create an office layout that meets individual work needs.

> "[During the pandemic], I learned the importance of a dedicated space instead of setting up on the dining room table."

❖ **Family-proof it.** If there is not enough space to create a home office location that's far enough away from family activities, consider installing additional soundproofing. Using a "white sound" system (such as a fan) or wearing a headset can help block distracting noises. It also helps to establish clear interruption rules and agreements regarding noise volume.

❖ **Think ergonomics.** Choose furnishings (desk, chair, computer table, etc.) that are conducive to efficient work. Ensure that the workspace has both task lighting and ambient lighting, and that there's a source of ventilation and temperature control.

❖ **Keep it organized.** Keep the home office as tidy as a traditional, on-site office. Keep it clean and free of clutter with easy access to needed resources.

FINAL THOUGHTS

This chapter has addressed some of the thornier difficulties associated with remote work. Even with adequate planning, thoughtful remote worker selection and preparation, and well-equipped leaders, there are complexities that require new solutions to unique problems and new responses to evolving situations.

> **"The best do well working almost anywhere, but ...[remote work] requires significant work and time from leaders."**

As we've seen, activating remote work "on the fly" is fraught with complications and frustrations. So, if the organization has not yet switched to remote operations, stay prepared. Ensure that team members are mission-ready and ask them to begin assembling the resources to allow the business to survive—in the very likely reality of a virtual workplace that is here to stay.

AFTERWORD

There's no doubt that remote leaders will continue facing new challenges and potential barriers to success for themselves and their teams as the virtual workplace expands. We've identified and provided solutions for many of the obstacles leaders have shared with us as we've worked with them and heard through interviews and surveys we conducted in preparing to write this book. We believe that none of these obstacles are insurmountable, particularly if leaders utilize the coaching guidelines and relationship skills we've discussed throughout these chapters.

We hope that the information we've gathered and the tools we've shared will arm remote leaders to tackle the barriers to success they face. And we also hope that leaders will effectively engage their expanding work-from-anywhere teams and fluid hybrid teams. The real key to remote leadership success is to leverage the energy and ideas of team members who are likely to have a deep commitment to ensuring that the virtual workplace is one that works well for them, their leaders, and their organizations.

We wish you much success as you lead remotely and support your dispersed teams in achieving high performance from a distance.

APPENDICES

A

ICEBREAKERS FOR VIRTUAL TEAM MEETINGS

Most traditional icebreakers can be used in a virtual environment with slight modifications. Here are a variety of icebreaker exercises to use with teams or project groups.

ICE BREAKER	STANDARD PLAY	VIRTUAL TEAM VERSION
QUESTION GAME	Participants write a thought-provoking question (or 2 or 3 questions) they would like to ask others in the group, i.e. "Where is the most interesting place you've ever traveled?" or "What would you be doing if money were no object?" People are given time to mingle and ask others their questions. When they get back together, each person can introduce one of the people they've met to the broader group.	It's hard to mingle in a virtual meeting, but there are alternative ways to implement the virtual version of this game. Using the breakout room option in the meeting app, sort people into pairs or small groupings. Alternatively, participants can use instant messaging or online chat to reach out to one another. If the group size is fairly small, have each participant type their question, then have each person share their screen with their question. Ask every participant to answer the question on the screen. Continue through all questions and all participants.

ICE BREAKER	STANDARD PLAY	VIRTUAL TEAM VERSION
MAP GAME	Hang a large map of the world (or country) and give everyone a pushpin. As people enter the room, ask them to pin the location of their favorite place to vacation (or place they most want to go for vacation) to the map.	This is easy to replicate with most desktop sharing apps. Show an image of a world or country map and have participants annotate where they would like to go on their dream vacation – or ask one participant to "manage the map" by annotating responses.
ARTIST GAME	Participants have 5 minutes to draw a picture with paper and pen that best conveys who they are without writing any words or numbers. The facilitator collects the pictures and then shows each drawing, one at a time, to the group. Everyone has a minute to guess who drew it. Each artist then is given a few minutes to explain how the work conveys who they are.	Participants have a few minutes to go to the Web and find an image or screenshot that best conveys who they are and emails the image to the meeting facilitator. The facilitator or team leader shares each image on the screen one at a time, and participants try to guess who submitted it. Participants are each given the opportunity to explain why they chose their selected image.

ICE BREAKER	STANDARD PLAY	VIRTUAL TEAM VERSION
PICTIONARY	The facilitator gives a group member a word, phrase, or movie title. The participant tries to communicate the word by drawing pictures without using any numbers or letters.	The facilitator sends a word, phrase, or movie title to a participant through instant messenger or chat. The participant shares their screen in the meeting app and tries to communicate the word or phrase by using emoticons, drawing using the annotation functionality, or using photos.
THREE IN COMMON GAME	The group is split into smaller groups of three people each. Each small group is tasked with finding three (or a designated number you choose) things they have in common. The commonalities should be interesting or unique things (not things like age, sex, hair color, etc.). After five minutes, the large group reconvenes, and each small group briefs the rest of the participants.	This can be played in a similar way as the face-to-face version by using the breakout room function in the meeting app.

ICE BREAKER	STANDARD PLAY	VIRTUAL TEAM VERSION
THREE TRUTHS AND A LIE	Each member of the group writes four statements about themselves. Three of the statements must be true, and one is not. The facilitator reads each of the statements and the group tries to guess which one is not true.	Each participant types their statements in a document on their computer. The participants take turns sharing their screens and displaying their statements. The rest of the team can guess out loud or use the polling function in the meeting app to guess which statement is not true.
PARTICIPANT BINGO	Before the meeting, make a Bingo matrix. In each square, write something that most or some of the participants have or have not likely done (i.e. visited another country, never felt snow, etc.). Randomize the Bingo cards and hand out to participants. Each person asks questions of others and fills in the name of someone that meets the criteria for a given Bingo square. The first person to get a "Bingo" (all	Create the Bingo cards and email them to participants at the beginning of the meeting. Participants will have to use the chat, instant message, or text to ask others their questions. The first person to get a Bingo notifies the facilitator or uses the meeting app emoticons to signal that they've won.

	names across a column or row), wins.	
TRAPPED ON A DESERT ISLAND	The group is divided into smaller groups, and each group is given the same scenario: They have just crash landed on a remote desert island and can only choose three items from the burning plane. They are provided with a list of potential survival items, such as a compass, needle and thread, box of matches, mirror, etc. After the small groups pick their items, they reconvene as the large group and explain why they chose their three items. There's no right or wrong answer; the purpose is to get the team to work together, understand each other's perspectives, and make decisions.	This icebreaker can be easily replicated using the breakout room functionality in most meeting applications. If the meeting app doesn't have that capability, the facilitator provides everyone with the scenario, shows the list of items on the screen, and participants vote using the polling feature or use the chat capability to indicate which items they would choose. The facilitator then asks each participant to explain the reasoning behind their choices.

ICE BREAKER	VIRTUAL TEAM VERSION
TAKE A POLL	The polling functionality found in most meeting apps provides facilitators with a simple way to survey participants and break the ice at the beginning of a meeting or to keep participants engaged throughout the meeting. Meeting leaders can ask anything including how everyone is feeling about a particular subject, things they would like to do, or opinions on certain ideas. Once everyone has taken the poll, the meeting leader shares the results and asks follow-up questions or facilitates group discussion.
HOME OFFICE TREASURE HUNT	Give participants a few minutes to find the strangest thing in their home office. (You can adapt this to have participants find the most meaningful item instead.) They can each hold up the item on video and explain what it is and the meaning behind it.
SHARE A PHOTO	Using the screen sharing function, participants share a photo from their device. For example, the meeting leader can have participants select a fun, silly, or special photo in the gallery and share with the team.

Find additional icebreaker ideas on the Internet that can encourage interaction or energize a team meeting. With a little additional thought and minimal effort, these games and discussion stimulators can be effectively adapted for your virtual team gatherings.

B

SAMPLE INTERVIEW QUESTIONS TO EXPLORE READINESS/PREFERENCE FOR REMOTE WORK

Below are sample interview questions that might help generate discussion about a remote position and identify potential obstacles, concerns, needs for support, and coaching opportunities. These sample questions can be used to supplement competency-based questions that focus on the skills required for a selected position. You don't have to ask them all, and this is not an all-inclusive list. You can be inspired by these to create questions that are more directly relevant to the position.

1. **What has been your experience working remotely (even if part-time) or working with remote team members?**

2. **Why do you want to work remotely?**
   (Prior to COVID-19, this question was often used as a "gotcha" question. If a candidate said they wanted to work from home because they didn't have any childcare, then employers were less likely to allow the person to work from home because the company didn't want the person to be distracted. During the pandemic, with the shutdown of schools, this question became irrelevant. Following the pandemic, employers might be more inclined to confirm a reasonable and appropriate division between work and childcare activities.)

3. What are the differences between the way you work remotely and the way you work in an office? What are the positives and negatives of each situation for you personally?

4. What is your biggest strength when it comes to working remotely or working with remote team members?

5. When you have worked remotely, how did you structure your day? Did you use any tools, apps, or systems to help you?

6. How do you prioritize work activities?

7. If you had a technical problem and couldn't reach the help desk, how would you solve it?

8. What type of support (both technical and from your manager) do you expect while you are working remotely?

9. What kind of distractions did you encounter while working remotely? How did you typically handle it?

10. How do you stay motivated when you can't see others in-person?

11. How do you set the boundaries between work and home life when you are working from home?

12. Tell me about your physical home workspace. Do you share it with others? If yes, how do you manage conflicts, distractions, and shared space?

13. What are the things present in your home office that help you do your job?

14. What's the one thing in your home office that makes you the most productive?

15. If you are not physically located with a co-worker, how would you be able to determine if the co-worker had a problem working with you? How would you resolve it?

16. What are your biggest concerns about working remotely?

17. What's your preferred method(s) and tools that you use to communicate and collaborate with others you can't meet face-to-face?

18. How would you prepare and facilitate meetings with others when some team members might be physically together while others are remote?

19. (Situational) You are leading a team effort with some members co-located with you and others that are 100 percent remote. How do you ensure you have engagement from everyone on the team?

20. (Situational) You are asked to lead a brainstorming session to solve a problem. Everyone is remote and can't meet face-to-face. How would you lead the session? What tools and techniques would you use?

C

DIGITAL COMMUNICATION ASSESSMENT

Use this Digital Communication Assessment with team members to evaluate and clarify use of technology tools and to establish guidelines, expectations, and agreements for effective communication with the team, project, or organization.

STEP	ACTION
1	**IDENTIFY ALL POTENTIAL TOOLS AVAILABLE TO THE TEAM FOR COMMUNICATION** (i.e. email, phone, text, instant messaging, video messaging, video meetings, etc.)
2	**WITH INPUT FROM YOUR TEAM, ESTABLISH TEAM NORMS ON WHAT TYPE OF INFORMATION SHOULD BE COMMUNICATED BY EACH METHOD.** For example, "text messaging/calls to a team member's mobile phone is only done for immediate, business critical information."
3	**IDENTIFY EXPECTED RESPONSE TIMES.** For example, text messages require immediate response (drop what you are doing and respond), instant messaging requires a response as soon as the team member can tend to it, email responses will vary (urgency should be expressed in the subject line), etc.

4	**DEFINE ANY STANDARDS OF LENGTH.** For example, text messages/instant messaging should be less than 2 sentences or 50 characters, otherwise it should be in an email. Voicemails should be under 1 minute, otherwise set up time to discuss, etc.
5	**DEFINE ANY LIMITATIONS OR RESTRICTIONS.** For example, no calls or texts on weekends.
6	**IDENTIFY REPOSITORIES OR SHARED INFORMATION SITES AND HOW OFTEN THE TEAM SHOULD ACCESS THEM.**
7	**IDENTIFY ANY ADDITIONAL COMMUNICATION ETIQUETTE RULES, SUCH AS WHO SHOULD OR SHOULD NOT BE COPIED ON VARIOUS TYPES OF COMMUNICATION.**

Summarize details in a communication matrix and communicate throughout the organization or team.

Example follows

— Example —

DIGITAL COMMUNICATION MATRIX

METHOD	PURPOSE	EXPECTED RESPONSE TIME	LENGTH	RESTRICTIONS	NOTES
EMAIL	Various	Should be specified in subject line	Should be able to read the email without scrolling	n/a	Subject line says... "URGENT" = 2-hour response "IMPORTANT" = same day response
VIDEO MEETING	Project meetings, team meetings	Should be specified in invite	varies		Try to provide at least 2-hour advance notice to prepare
IN-PERSON MEETING	Performance reviews, coaching, team building	Should be specified in invite	varies		Try to provide at least 1-day notice for team member to be in office
TEAM SITE	Policies, large files, general info	n/a	n/a	No sensitive information	Check daily

— Example —

DIGITAL COMMUNICATION MATRIX

METHOD	PURPOSE	EXPECTED RESPONSE TIME	LENGTH	RESTRICTIONS	NOTES
EMAIL	Various	Should be specified in subject line	Should be able to read the email without scrolling	n/a	Subject line says... "URGENT" = 2-hour response "IMPORTANT" = same day response
VIDEO MEETING	Project meetings, team meetings	Should be specified in invite	varies		Try to provide at least 2-hour advance notice to prepare
IN-PERSON MEETING	Performance reviews, coaching, team building	Should be specified in invite	varies		Try to provide at least 1-day notice for team member to be in office
TEAM SITE	Policies, large files, general info	n/a	n/a	No sensitive information	Check daily

Virtual Meeting Checklist

Before the meeting:

☐ Plan the **agenda**.

☐ **Distribute** the agenda and information in advance; confirm receipt.

☐ Clarify **responsibilities** (for notetaking, timekeeping, meeting leadership, technical support) for the meeting.

☐ Identify the appropriate/desired **technology** to be used. Confirm the availability/accessibility of the selected technology for all participants.

☐ Arrange for **required equipment, information, and people** to be involved.

☐ **Test** the technology. Make sure that things work ahead of time so you can minimize wasting people's time with techno-glitches.

During the meeting:

☐ Encourage everyone to **introduce** themselves (or verbally "sign in") at the beginning of the meeting and **identify** themselves whenever they speak (except for video/web conferencing or well-established teams whose voices are recognized by everyone).

☐ Establish **expectations for involvement** by all participants (periodically pause to summarize and ask for questions, discussion, clarification).

☐ Ensure that **visual or graphic resources** can be distributed "real-time" or in advance to everyone (via e-mail, download, network access, shared document site, etc.).

☐ Remind everyone to **speak slowly, clearly** and in the direction of microphones/speakerphones or on remote phone; request that something be repeated if not heard clearly.

☐ Suggest that participants wear headsets if joining remotely and use the **"Mute" option** on their phones to eliminate background noise that might be disruptive to a virtual meeting.

☐ Keep to the **schedule**.

After the meeting:

☐ Distribute **meeting summary** in a timely manner, with details regarding agreements and follow-up actions.

☐ Schedule any **follow-up meetings** needed.

☐ Implement any **action steps** that were agreed to during the meeting.

☐ Solicit **feedback** from participants on how similar meetings in the future can be enhanced/improved.

Download the Virtual Meeting Checklist:

www.virtualworkswell.com/checklist

REFERENCES

Chapter 1

Wilson, J., Straus, S., McEvily, B. "All in due time: The development of trust in computer-mediated and face-to-face teams." Organizational Behavior and Human Decision Processes. Volume 99, Issue 1, January 2006, pp 16-33. https://doi.org/10.1016/j.obhdp.2005.08.001

Griffis, Hailley. (2017, August 1). "The 5 Ways We Build Trust on a Fully Remote Team and Why It's So Valuable." Buffer.com. https://buffer.com/resources/trust-remote-team/#:~:text=Intentionally%20getting%20to%20know%20eac h,are%20powerful%20in%20creating%20trust.&text=Being%20 remote%20means%20that%20we,grabbing%20a%20cup%20of %20coffee.

Dinnocenzo, Debra. (2006). How to Lead From a Distance. Dallas, TX: The Walk The Talk Co.

Chapter 2

Goodheart, Adam. (2000, July 26). USA Today.

TechTarget. (2020). *Virtual Presence.* https://whatis.techtarget.com/definition/virtual-presence

Dinnocenzo, Debra. (2006). How to Lead From a Distance. Dallas, TX: The Walk The Talk Co.

Chapter 4

Lucas, Suzanne. "Why You Might Want to Hire Your Next Employee Before You Meet Her." Inc. https://www.inc.com/suzanne-lucas/more-businesses.-are-hiring-sight-unseen.html. Last modified Nov 18, 2019

Trull, Samuel G. "Strategies of Effective Interviewing." Harvard Business Review. https://hbr.org/1964/01/strategies-of-effective-interviewing

Gartner. "Gartner CFO Survey Reveals 74% Intend to Shift Some Employees to Remote Work Permanently." April 3, 2020. https://www.gartner.com/en/newsroom/press-releases/2020-04-03-gartner-cfo-surey-reveals-74-percent-of-organizations-to-shift-some-employees-to-remote-work-permanently2

Laurano, Madeline. "The True Cost of Bad Hire." Glassdoor, last modified August 2015. https://b2b-assets.glassdoor.com/the-true-cost-of-a-bad-hire.pdf
Hirsch, Arlene S. "Don't Underestimate the Importance of Good Onboarding." SHRM.org, last modified August 10, 2017. https://www.shrm.org/resourcesandtools/hr-topics/talent-acquisition/pages/dont-underestimate-the-importance-of-effective-onboarding.aspx

"State of the American Workplace", Gallup, https://www.gallup.com/workplace/238085/state-american-workplace-report-2017.aspx

Filipkowski, Jenna. "Talent Pulse", Human Capital Institute, last modified June 22, 2016 http://www.hci.org/files/field_content_file/2016%20Talent%20Pulse%20TA.pdf

Zoe, Eleni. "Satisfaction with Onboarding: What New Hires Want", TalentLMS.com, last modified August 22, 2019.

Chapter 5

Dinnocenzo, Debra. (2006). How to Lead From a Distance. Dallas, TX: The Walk The Talk Co.

Chapter 6

Robbins, Stephen P. Organizational Behavior. Pearson Education, Inc. Upper Saddle River, NJ. 2003. pp. 524-525

Watkins, Michael D. "What Is Organizational Culture? And Why Should We Care?" May 15, 2013. https://hbr.org/2013/05/what-is-organizational-culture

CULTURE OVER CASH? GLASSDOOR MULTI-COUNTRY SURVEY FINDS MORE THAN HALF OF EMPLOYEES PRIORITIZE WORKPLACE CULTURE OVER SALARY, https://about-content.glassdoor.com/en-us/workplace-culture-over-salary/

"3 Examples of Great Organizational Culture You Can Learn From." September 21, 2016. https://www.indeed.com/lead/build-great-organizational-culture

[1] https://www.grocerydive.com/news/grocery--a-grocery-stores-average-annual-turnover-cost-is-67k-says-consultant/534692/

Patel, Sujan. "10 Examples of Companies With Fantastic Cultures." Entrepreneur. August 6, 2015. https://www.entrepreneur.com/article/249174

Ungarino, Rebecca. "Uber tanked 11% after logging the biggest first-day dollar loss in US IPO history." Business Insider. May 13, 2019. https://markets.businessinsider.com/news/stocks/uber-technologies-inc-stock-falls-after-brutal-ipo-2019-5-1028195064#

Heathfield, Susan M. "Find Out How Zappos Reinforces Its Company Culture." July 30, 2019. https://www.thebalancecareers.com/zappos-company-culture-1918813

MacFarland, Keith. "Why Zappos Offers New Hires $2,000 to Quit." https://www.redstrategygroup.com/insights/2016/2/26/why-zappos-offers-new-hires-2000-to-quit

Nisen, Max. "Zappos Is Building An Intentionally Inconvenient Office In Downtown Las Vegas." Business Insider. March 15, 2013. https://www.businessinsider.com/zappos-new-downtown-las-vegas-office-2013-3

Vasel, Kathryn. "How Zappos is trying to keep remote workers sane: Herb gardens and confetti (seriously)." CNN Business. August 20,2020. https://www.cnn.com/2020/08/20/success/zappos-office-culture-remote-workers/index.html

Dill, Kathryn. "It's Not Just Working Remotely; Hiring and Onboarding Go Virtual, Too." The Wall Street Journal. April 15, 2020. https://www.wsj.com/articles/its-not-just-working-remotely-hiring-and-onboarding-go-virtual-too-11586963419

Mann, Annmarie. "Why We Need Best Friends at Work." January 15, 2018. https://www.gallup.com/workplace/236213/why-need-best-friends-work.aspx

Christoffersen, Trish. "How To Keep Company Culture In A Remote Worker's World." January 9, 2020. https://www.zappos.com/about/stories/culture-fit-remote-workers

Chapter 7

Tajfel, H. and Turner, J.C. (1979), "An integrative theory of intergroup behavior", in Austin, W.G. and Worchel, S. (Eds), The Social Psychology of Intergroup Relations, Brooks/Cole, Monterey, CA, pp. 33-47.

Ellemers, N., Sleebos, E., Stam, D. and de Gilder, D. (2013), "Feeling included and valued: how perceived respect affects positive team identity and willingness to invest in the team", British Journal of Management, Vol. 24 No. 1, pp. 21-37

Box, N., Olson, J., Gergle, D., Olson, G., & Wright, Z. (2002). Effects of four computer-mediated communications channels on trust development. In Proc. SIGCHI.

Mullen, Brian, Johnson, Craig, and Salas, Eduardo. "Productivity Loss in Brainstorming Groups: A Meta-Analytic

Integration." Published online: 07 Jun 2010.
https://doi.org/10.1207/s15324834basp1201_1
Markman, Art. "Your Team Is Brainstorming All Wrong."
Harvard Business Review. May 18, 2017.
https://hbr.org/2017/05/your-team-is-brainstorming-all-wrong

Burke, Kelly and Chidambaram, Laku. "Do Mediated
Contexts Differ in Information Richness?
A Comparison of Collocated and Dispersed Meetings."
Proceedings of the 29th Annual Hawaii International
Conference on System Sciences. February 1996.

Chapter 8

BYU Communications. "Telecommuters with flextime
stay balanced up to 19 hours longer." May 31, 2020.
https://news.byu.edu/news/telecommuters-flextime-stay-balanced-19-hours-longer

DEBRA A. DINNOCENZO

Debra A. Dinnocenzo is a dynamic speaker, successful author, seasoned executive, and innovative educator with more than three decades of experience in the human resources industry. As a nationally recognized expert in the virtual workplace, Debra has written, consulted, trained, and presented keynote addresses on remote leadership,  virtual teams, and telework over the past two decades. She is the author several books, including *How to Lead From a Distance, Working From a Distance: Being Your Best When You're Not With the Rest, Managing Telecommuters, 101 Tips for Telecommuters,* and *Emergency Telecommuting.* Her books on work-life balance include *Dot Calm: The Search for Sanity in a Wired World* and *Working Too Much Can Make You Grumpy.* Debra is a member of the National Speakers Association and is an experienced keynote speaker.

Debra has worked with a wide range of corporations, industries, and government entities to implement telework programs, prepare managers to lead from a distance, and equip teams to work well together in the virtual workplace. Since publishing her first book on telecommuting in 1999, Debra has been a pioneer in the shift to virtual work and remote leadership. Few practitioners in the field have the depth of knowledge and hand-on experience Debra brings to her work.

Debra held consulting, product management, sales leadership, and marketing positions with Development Dimensions International, Learning International, and Ridge Associates, in addition to leading VirtualWorks!, the training & consulting firm she founded in 1995. Debra has worked with executives, senior-level teams, and a variety of line employee groups, demonstrating versatility and skill with diverse groups. Debra also has extensive experience in delivery of training in the classroom and in adaptation of training to virtual environments utilizing a variety of web-based platforms.

An active member of her community, Debra also holds several leadership positions. She has served on the board of directors of the national AAA (American Automobile Association); is past chair of East Central AAA and currently serves as a director on the East Central AAA governing board; serves on the board of trustees of University of Pittsburgh Medical Center Passavant Hospital and St. Margaret Hospital; and is a member of the board of directors and secretary of the Passavant Hospital Foundation. Debra has served on the faculty of the Institute for Management Studies, the Lehigh University/ Iacocca Institute Global Village, and the special studies program at Chautauqua Institution. She held an adjunct faculty position with Duquesne University and delivered the online graduate course "Leadership in the Virtual Workplace" for seven years.

Debra holds Bachelor of Science and Master of Arts degrees in Management from Central Michigan University and is currently pursuing a Doctorate in Business Administration. She lives near Pittsburgh, PA.

debra@debradinnocenzo.com
www.DinnocenzoSpeaks.com
www.VirtualWorksWell.com
www.remoteleadershipbook.com

JASON MORWICK

Jason Morwick is a consultant and author who writes about remote working, leading in the virtual workplace, and business process improvement. Jason is co-author of the book *Workshift: Future-Proof Your Organization for the 21st Century* (Palgrave Macmillan, 2013), a handbook for organizations transitioning into the virtual workplace. He is also co-author of *Making Telework Work: Leading People and Leveraging Technology for High-impact Results* (Nicholas Brealey Publishing, 2009), a guide for managers and leaders on creating a case for telework and managing remote workers. He has published in journals, magazines, and websites such as *Quality Progress, Review of Business, Business Journal, Strategic HR Review, American Business Review, iSixSigma Magazine,* and isixsigma.com. Jason is also the co-author of *Gridiron Leadership: Winning Strategies and Breakthrough Tactics* (Praeger, 2009) and contributing author to *Six Sigma Software Quality Improvement* (McGraw-Hill, 2011).

As a founding member of the consulting company, FlexWork Global, Jason helped organizations design strategies, implement program plans and train leaders and employees as they prepared to transition to the modern, flexible workplace. His past clients included Thomson Reuters, Tufts Health Plan, and Blue Cross Blue Shield.

Jason is a graduate of the United States Military Academy at West Point. He is a former Army officer and earned a Master of Business Administration degree from Regis University, Denver, Colorado. Jason has managed teams in a variety of industries from hospitality to supply chain to technology to finance while working for companies such as Cisco Systems, Wyndham, and General Electric. He has focused on business process improvement and project management. Jason is a Six Sigma Master Black Belt and certified Project Management Professional (PMP). He has worked in a variety of positions including Six Sigma Master Black Belt, Program Manager; Director of Human Resources; and Director of Industrial Engineering. Jason has trained thousands of employees in Six Sigma, Diversity, Project Management, Communication Skills, Remote Working/Telework, and Leadership.

Jay@elpadvantage.com

www.remoteleadershipbook.com

MORE INFORMATION

If you're interested in:

❑ Ordering additional copies of this book

❑ Additional information and resources related to remote leadership, virtual teams, or virtual workplace solutions

❑ Scheduling a seminar, workshop, webinar, online training, presentation, or keynote address on topics addressed in this book

❑ Scheduling a thirty-minute complimentary consult via phone or video meeting

 Visit our website:

www.remoteleadershipbook.com

CONNECT WITH Virtual Works!

www.virtualworkswell.com

info@virtualworkswell.com

724.934.9349

facebook.com/virtualworkswell

www.virtualworkswell.com/signup.aspx

CONNECT WITH THE AUTHORS:

Debra A. Dinnocenzo

✉ debra@debradinnocenzo.com

in linkedin.com/in/debradinnocenzo

🐦 twitter.com/debradinnocenzo

🎤 www.dinnocenzospeaks.com

Jason Morwick

✉ Jay@elpadvantage.com

in linkedin.com/in/jason-morwick

🐦 twitter.com/JasonMorwick

—NOTES—

Made in the USA
Monee, IL
16 July 2021

73733001R00131